Life on the Edge of the Arctic Ocean

Teena Helmericks

Fathom Publishing Company
Anchorage, Alaska

ISBN 978-1-954896-23-9 Hardbound
ISBN 978-1-954896-24-6 Paperback
ISBN 978-1-954896-25-3 E-book

Library of Congress Control Number 2023913539
Printed in United States of America
First Edition

Credits: Image frames, depositphotos.com/MaryLev
The following trademarked product names are used with the permission of the trademark owner:
Carolina Skiff
Cessna
Grumman Sportsman
John Deere
Piper Super Cub

Publisher's Cataloging-in-Publication data
Names: Helmericks, Teena, author.
Title: Life on the edge of the Arctic Ocean / Teena Helmericks.
Description: Includes index. | Anchorage, AK: Fathom Publishing Company, 2023.
Identifiers: LCCN: 2023913539 | ISBN: 978-1-954896-23-9 (hardcover) | 978-1-954896-24-6 (paperback) | 978-1-954896-25-3 (ebook)
Subjects: LCSH Helmericks, Teena. | Utqiaġvik (Alaska)–Biography. | Utqiaġvik (Alaska)–Social life and customs. | Barrow (Alaska)–Biography. | Alaska–Biography. | BISAC BIOGRAPHY & AUTOBIOGRAPHY / Personal Memoirs | BIOGRAPHY & AUTOBIOGRAPHY / Aviation & Nautical | BIOGRAPHY & AUTOBIOGRAPHY / Women
Classification: LCC F910.7.H46 2023 | DDC 979.8/052092–dc23

fathompublishing.com
Fathom Publishing Company
P.O. Box 200448
Anchorage, Alaska 99520-0448
Telephone /Fax 907-272-3305

Dedication

To my husband Jim
and our four sons,
Derek, Jay, Isaac, and Aaron

Contents

List of Illustrations

Utqiaġvik

The northernmost community in the United States sits near the tip of Alaska on the Arctic Ocean. It resides at the transition point between the Chukchi Sea to the west and the Beaufort Sea to the east.

This is the land of the Iñupiat people who have inhabited the coastline for thousands of years. They called their village Utqiaġvik.

In 1826, a Royal Navy officer, Frederick W. Beechey, was sent to explore and map the Arctic coastline of North America. He named the northernmost point for Sir John Barrow, Second Secretary to the Admiralty. The village of Utqiaġvik was located a short distance east from the point and so became known as Barrow.

The name Barrow remained in use until 2016, when the town citizens voted to reinstate the village's traditional Iñupiaq name: Utqiaġvik. This was an important step honoring the Iñupiat culture and boosting use of the language.

The first section of the book covers the author's childhood growing up in this wonderful village in the 1950s. Remaining chapters detail the years she and her husband raised four boys, fishing, hunting, and exploring the Arctic along the Colville River Delta. Barrow was the name in use during these events and is therefore used throughout the book.

The author and publisher wish to honor the return of Utqiaġvik and recognize it as the correct and current name.

Acknowledgements

Thank you to my husband, Jim, with whom I've shared over fifty years of Colville Homestead life. Many thanks for sharing his many excellent photos and his assistance in keeping facts and figures accurate for this book.

I appreciate my four sons, Derek, Jay, Isaac, and Aaron, who lived this life with Jim and me. They always found people's curiosity over their lives peculiar since it was simply our way of life which was ordinary to them. I love you all so much!

To all my family and friends who unrelentingly encouraged me to write down the stories of my life in Arctic Alaska, I hope you find this work full of answers to your many questions. I appreciate the love and support from you all.

I have many people to thank for all the help and encouragement given me over the years to promote the writing and publishing this book. Other than all my family and many friends, there are a few I want to especially mention.

Special thanks goes to my sister-in-law, Denise Wartes, who was persistent in giving me both encouragement and technical guidance over many years, especially when I would bog down for long periods when multiple home duties and outside jobs distracted me.

Thanks to my friend Clive Beckmann for giving me a much needed boost with early-on editing.

Thanks to my many friends and colleagues in my oil field jobs who persistently asked the questions about my unusual family life and wanted me to tell them more. "You have to write a book," they would say! Here you are—this is for you.

Lastly, much credit goes to Connie Taylor, my publisher, who helped me organize and edit my stories. Her expertise and guidance gave me the final thrust to pull everything together and create this book. Thank you, Connie, so much!

Introduction

It has not been easy to pull together stories and descriptions of my unusual life, but I have continually been encouraged to write and share these experiences. What started as a few stories has developed into more of an autobiography and memoir.

Therefore, the stories and lifestyle descriptions in this book try to answer the main questions about me and my family's Arctic lives. So many questions: When, Where, How, and most often, Why?

My unique Alaskan lifestyle began in childhood in Barrow, the northernmost community in the United States. This upbringing in an Arctic village later prepared me for and greatly influenced my family life on the edge of the Arctic Ocean where it butts up against the Colville River Delta.

Life here in the Arctic has always been a challenge for my family—a life of struggles against the harsh elements, extremely hard work, developing self-taught construction and mechanical skills, and long periods of isolation from extended family and friends. Yet through it all, there has been joy and satisfaction in overcoming these hardships, and pride in all my family's accomplishments reached through industriousness, ingenuity, and resourcefulness. Together we have built a remarkable life of freedom, independence, and value.

Overlaying it all has been trust in God's care and His benevolence in all circumstances. Besides this, my husband, Jim, and I have had to have unrelenting confidence in each other through it all. After a brief stay with us, a guest once told us, "You live on the edge of disaster all the time!" He went on to explain how he saw our lives. "You are so dependent on each other that if some misfortune took one of you away, the other could not survive here long." That is probably true, but with the grace of God and much perseverance, we continue life on the Colville. We have maintained a three-generation homestead, added many buildings and improvements, developed businesses, and raised our children in a land few ever see, let alone experience first-hand.

A big contributing factor to our successful homestead lifestyle at such a unique location can be traced back to both my husband Jim's and my childhoods. I grew up in the Arctic with no childhood memories of any other place and it was naturally home for me. Jim started his life as a young Colorado farm boy who quickly adapted his childhood experiences to Arctic life. We both had amazing parents that infused us with uncompromising love and fierceness for dealing with whatever life threw at us. Therefore, I feel it is appropriate to include in this saga some backgrounds from us both.

Teena Helmericks

Spring 2023

Our homestead on Anachlik Island, looking north.

Where We Live

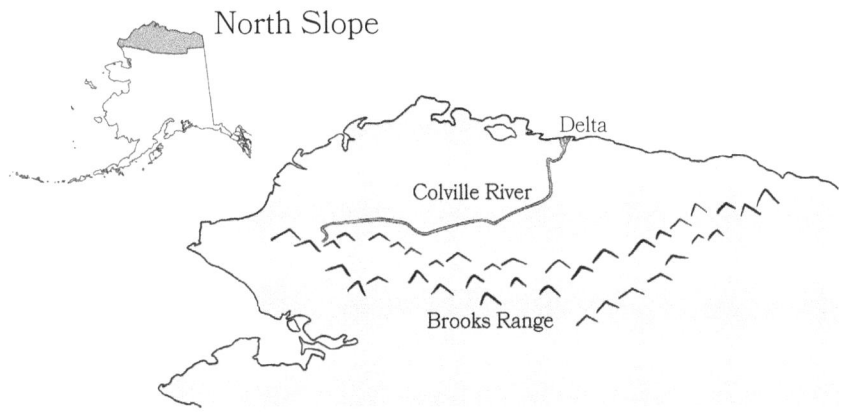

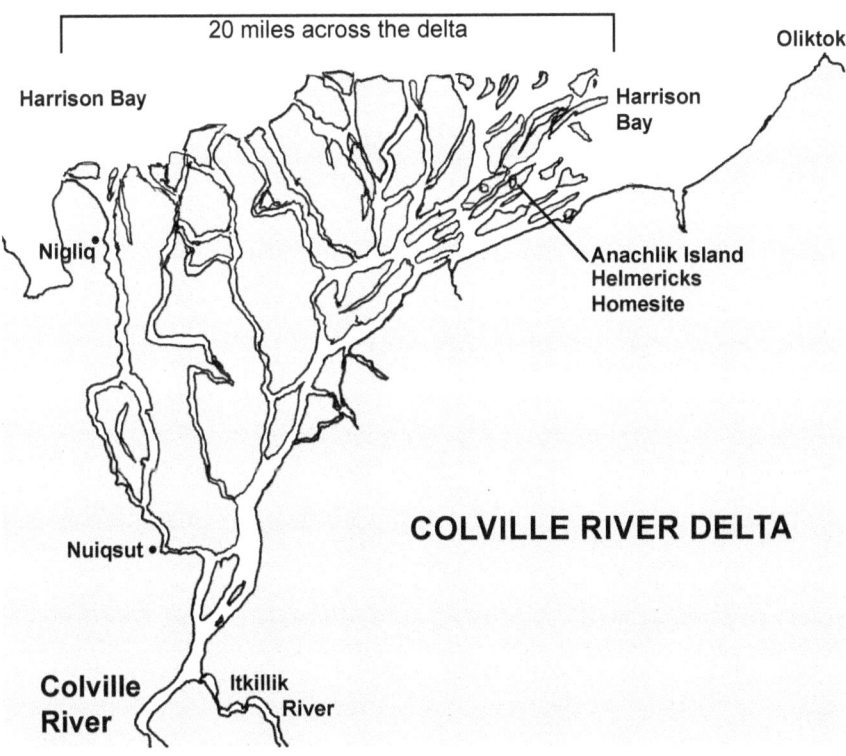

The Delta is full of small lakes and streams not shown here on the map as well as many sandbars and dunes. Only a few of the channels are navigable. It is prime waterfowl habitat with nutritious salt grasses along the face of the Delta.

Prelude:
Lost in a Whiteout

I was lost in a white world! It was slightly above 0°F and a SW wind was driving snow into my face so hard that my visibility was seriously limited by icy snow crystals striking my eyes like painful needles. I couldn't wear my snow goggles since they impeded my visibility even more.

I had been following a trail, but the visibility was so bad I had suddenly lost the trail with a blink of the eyes. I swerved back and forth trying to find the older snowmachine track again. It was nowhere to be seen. I knew I was in trouble.

I admit that the trail from the start was only visible for a few feet in front of me, but I thought I could stay on track, not knowing the wind and blowing snow would continue to increase, cutting visibility practically to nil. Maybe I should have turned back at that point.

I had started this rigorous snowmachine drive from our end-of-road access point to our remote homestead home in the Colville River Delta. I made the drive twice a month as I left and returned home from my oil field job. There were no roads all the way home, so I had to use my snowmobile, or as we call them in Alaska, a snowmachine, to get across the final five miles of tundra and frozen river channels. I was dressed in my fur parka and other cold-weather gear.

After two weeks of intense twelve-hour days, seven days a week work, I was super eager to get home. My husband, Jim, waiting at home, had advised me to wait for better weather, but I was overly confident and stubborn. Now I was in a pickle.

I kept driving, thinking as long as I kept the wind in my face, I was at least headed in the right general direction and would come upon the trail again shortly. The minutes slipped away, and still no trail. I lost track of time, but knew I was far enough overdue getting home by then that Jim would be out searching for me. That gave me comfort, but also irritated me that I caused him worry and extra work. I should have followed his recommendation to wait for better weather.

Fatigue was setting in as I hung on to the handlebars of my snowmachine and lurched over incredibly rough snowdrifts. It had already been a long day, as I rose at 5 a.m. at work and had to drive my truck three to four hours to get to the jumping-off location where my parked snowmachine waited. My stamina was winding down, but I continued driving in increasingly bigger circles trying to find the trail I was supposed to be following. Jim was driving his snowmachine over the trail from our house when he caught a glimpse of my headlight bouncing along as I circled toward him. He turned and headed straight for me, at which point I saw his light appear out of the drifting snow.

I was found! Fortunately, God was with me that day as always and shortened my exhausting ordeal. Jim was able to lead me straight home with his superior sense of direction despite the increasing intensity of the storm. I had veered off-track by about twenty-five degrees and would have completely missed our house if I had continued in the direction I was headed. Thankfully, Jim had my back!

We keep strict protocol for dangerous traveling conditions with check-in times and rescue plans. It has served us well over the many years of travel across harsh and remote landscapes.

PART ONE

Beginnings – Up to 1970s

Aerial of Anachlik Island looking north with Arctic Ocean pack ice on the horizon. East channel of the Colville River in the foregound.

Chapter 1
My Early Years

Pre-Alaska Days

I was born in Seattle, Washington, on June 9, 1948. Bonnie and Bill Wartes named their third child a Biblical name they had liked from Sunday School days, Ascenath, with middle name Blanche after her paternal grandmother. Ascenath is Egyptian; this was the name of Joseph's wife, the high priest's daughter. Remember Joseph, the eleventh son of Jacob, who was sold into slavery by his ten older brothers? Joseph later rose from slavery to the highest position in Egypt under the pharaoh. The part of that story where Ascenath is mentioned is in the forty-first chapter of Genesis, and the name is spelled Asenath in the Bible.

My older brother Mark, three when I was born, could not pronounce Ascenath. His attempts to do so sounded like Tee-nah, this nickname stuck, and this is the name by which most people have known me all my life.

My mother and father were both raised in Seattle, graduated from Ballard High School, and attended the University of Washington. They married in 1942. Dad joined the Air Force in 1943 and was soon piloting B-24 bombers up and down

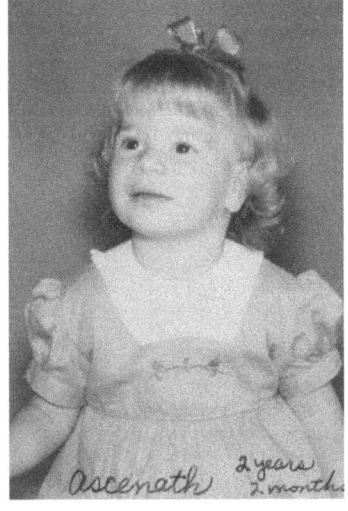

Teena pre-Alaskan days, 1950.

3

Teena with her brother Mark before moving to Barrow.

the Pacific coast on guard patrol. He also trained many other pilots during WWII. After the atomic bomb dropped on Hiroshima, Dad was honorably discharged from the service to continue his training in Christian ministry at the University of Washington and he pastored a church in Lakewood, Washington.

Just after I was born, we moved to Marin City, California, for Dad to attend San Anselmo Seminary for three years. Straight from

Wartes family before leaving Seattle for Alaska, 1951, left to right, Bill, Teena held by Bonnie, Mark, Merrily.

there, Mom and Dad accepted a missionary position in Barrow, Alaska, under the Presbyterian Board of National Missions. Dad was the ideal choice since a pastor was needed who could fly a brand-new mission airplane purchased for the northern Alaska mission field, plus Dad's carpentry experience was needed for the building of a new sanctuary. Building materials had already been shipped to Barrow and were stacked on the ocean beach. Dad was a pilot, an architect, and an ordained pastor willing to go to a mission field, a perfect match for Barrow.

Arriving in Barrow

I arrived in Barrow the summer of 1951. Our family of five, Mom and Dad, older sister and brother, Merrily and Mark, and I, left Seattle aboard a ship to Seward early July. From Seward to Fairbanks, we traveled by train. We boarded a DC-3 in Fairbanks. This large twin engine plane took us to Barrow, where we landed on the only large runway located east of Barrow at the Navy Arctic Research Lab (NARL). Samuel Simmonds, an exceptional Iñupiat man who would later become Dad's assistant and interpreter, met us at the airport with a tractor pulling a large open sled to carry us and all our belongings the six miles into Barrow. My mother loves to tell the story about my innocent remark while riding the sled into Barrow. I had casually said, "Back in the world, we had a red car."

So, at barely three years of age, forgetting any earlier memories, I became an Alaskan for life. The die was cast, and Alaska would always be my home.

My parents had always wanted to serve in a small community, somewhere on a mission field. They fit in quickly and loved Barrow and its friendly people. The Iñupiat people of Barrow were already well versed in the Christian faith from earlier missionaries, and the church was the focal point of the whole community. Dad was soon immersed in leading his new flock, directing the building of the new church sanctuary, and flying the new mission plane to outlying villages that had no in-house pastor.

Children playing in yard of the manse with church in center, 1950s.

Mother not only cared for her family, but also helped a great deal with church business, community record-keeping, and other church-related tasks such as teaching women's Bible studies. She had prepared well for supporting her family, who would be living far from stores and easily obtained goods, by ordering enough groceries and other household supplies to last a year before leaving Seattle. Most supplies needed in the furthest north community in North America had to arrive by one annual supply ship, the *North Star*. Mom had planned out meals and food quantities necessary to feed her family for more than a year at a time, and these supplies, having left Seattle by ship several months earlier, were to arrive in Barrow a month or so after we got there. We were soon a family of six. Mother was pregnant when we first arrived and my little sister Marti was born in January 1952.

My siblings and I were soon accepted into community life with all the other children. Wearing new fur parkas and other warm outdoor clothing, we were hard to distinguish from any other local child. It wasn't long before we spoke the same Pig Latin as the other children—a mixture of the Iñupiaq language spattered with English. Most of the people could speak English quite well by the 1950s and only some older folks still had difficulty. Dad decided not to take the time away from his many other duties to learn to speak fluent Iñupiaq. Samuel would interpret sermons for the sake of the older people. Dad usually traveled with an Iñupiaq-speaking companion also, so he had help translating if necessary.

My life became wrapped up in super-warm fur clothing, Iñupiat playmates, wonderful Iñupiat surrogate grandmas and aunts, and an enthralling land and traditions that would forever shape my life.

Childhood in Barrow

When we moved to Barrow, Mother brought lots of indoor games and activities for us children, being under the impression that there would be many months of winter that we wouldn't be able to go outdoors. However, that turned out not to be the case. With proper winter fur clothing, we played outdoors most of the time, even with temperatures well below zero.

I remember playing King-of-the-Mountain on huge pressure ridges of ice just off-shore Barrow on the frozen Arctic Ocean, building snow houses, and towing our small hand-sled around in the snow. There had to be a quite severe storm raging outside to keep us indoors.

My older brother Mark and I were practically inseparable in those early days. So from a very early age, I hung out with him and his other boyfriends, doing mostly boy-oriented activities like hunting games with our bows and arrows, shooting our BB guns, stocking imaginary game, and sledding. The whole village and surrounding land were an open playground. The Arctic prairie was forever woven into my blood as

Teena and Mark after playing in a snow storm, 1952.

my rightful homeland. I learned years later just how deeply embedded this love of the land had become. As I stepped off the plane the summer of 1965, returning to Barrow after a long absence, the poignant smell of the tundra brought tears of pleasure to my eyes. I hadn't even realized I had missed it so.

For many years in my younger days, I was quite ignorant about a lot of things most children are exposed to early on. For instance, I didn't know much about fresh fruit or vegetables. Once when a guest arriving from way south had brought some fresh vegetables as a gift, we kids began arguing over whether cabbage and lettuce were the same vegetable at different stages of growth. One of us said, "No, they are two different vegetables." After listening awhile, my younger brother Clayton piped up and said authoritatively, "Well, I know one thing for sure; they both grow on the same tree!"

Our family meals were filled with local fish and game brought to us by villagers or Dad and supplemented with canned or dried goods. Most store-bought supplies came once a year aboard the *North Star* cargo ship because air transportation was the only other way into Barrow and air freight was very expensive. Although Mom made lots of fresh bread, "Pilot Bread," a large round cracker and staple of Alaskan rural areas, was and still is one of my favorite foods. I learned to love many of the Iñupiat delicacies like raw frozen fish and meat called quaq, whale chunks called maktak, and smoked, dried fish called pivsi. Sometimes when I came up missing, Mom would find that I had snuck down into our underground deep-freeze cellar to munch on frozen meat or fish. Our cellar was dug deep into the permafrost under our porch and accessed through a trap door inside the porch floor.

Barrow had a population of about three hundred Iñupiat people in the 1950s, with only eight to ten white families or individuals manning a few posts: teaching positions, the weather bureau, hospital positions, and the Presbyterian mission.

Barrow was the largest Iñupiat community on the northern coast, but Dad's mission field also covered the smaller communities of Wainwright to the west and Kaktovik village on Barter Island, to the east. In addition to those established

The Manse in the foreground is where Wartes family lived in the 1950s. The hospital is the long building to the left.

villages, Dad would visit other people not in villages with his plane, the *Arctic Messenger*, including those living on the Colville River and families back in the mountains at what is now the village of Anaktuvuk Pass. He held services and conducted weddings and funerals all across the northern regions of Alaska. He and his plane also took part in many search and rescue operations and medical emergencies.

Alaska Flying Adventure

When Dad had to fly to Fairbanks for servicing the airplane, he would often take one of us kids along for the ride. I remember such a trip when I was chosen to be the privileged kid to go with Dad. It was the summer of 1956 and the great expanse of prairie (tundra) was green and splattered with small lakes and potholes that are held on the surface of the land by permafrost below. The *Arctic Messenger* was on floats, so we had enumerable landing sites below, if needed. We flew southeast, crossing the Colville River, and followed the Anaktuvuk River into the small village of Anaktuvuk Pass just inside the northern edge of the Brooks Range. We landed on the lake near the village, and I got my first visit with the folks there and saw first-hand one of the most beautiful spots in the Brooks Range. What a treat! The village sits at the true pass, where the headwaters of the Anaktuvuk and John Rivers begin and flow north and south respectively.

A few hours later we took off and continued south, down the John River to Bettles, where we landed in the Koyukuk River

Dad's plane the Arctic Messenger over the church in Barrow.

and fueled up. That was exciting since the river has a swift current at that location and the banks are higher than the top of the plane, so taxiing and maneuvering in fast moving water and getting safely anchored along a steep bank takes considerable skill.

Once safely tied up with the nose of the plane pointed upriver into the current, Dad had to walk up to the local store, buy his gas in five-gallon metal cans, and carry them back down to the plane. Fueling involved climbing up on a float, then the step that accessed the wing-top gas tank fill cap, and pouring the gas into the tank through the shammy-lined funnel.

Rev. William C. Wartes, missionary/pastor/pilot of the Presbyterian Mission in the 1950s supported the church name as the "Utkeaġvik Presbyterian Church," which is used to this day. The sign is constructed of bowhead whale bones. Now a new sign has the correct spelling: Utqiaġvik.

I scurried around exploring the river's edge and high bank while Dad fueled the plane. Everything was new and fascinating.

Leaving Bettles and crossing over more mountains gave Dad a chance for a nap. He instructed me to take the controls and keep the plane headed toward a certain mountain top, pointing at one in the distance ahead. Then I was to wake him when I got there, and he would point out the next landmark to which I was to fly. That was heady for an eight-year-old. I was puffed up with pride that Dad would trust me with steering the plane. Of course, in retrospect, I'm sure Dad secretly kept a pretty close eye on my progress through the sky.

As we flew high above the mighty Yukon River, the expanse of the world seemed to go on forever below us. The thick forests were a wonder to behold for a little girl used to the treeless plains of the Arctic.

Coming over the foothills north of Fairbanks and seeing such a big town ahead was another thrill ... looking down on all those buildings, roads, and vehicles was amazing to me. As we came in to land, Dad skirted between trees and over a bridge to land in the Chena Slough—an offshoot of the Chena River which gave Dad quick access to Bachners Aircraft Services, who serviced the plane.

As Dad took care of the plane, I wandered around the water's edge entranced by the trees, birds, and bugs so different from those at home on the Arctic coast. I remember being amazed at the huge dragonfly that landed on my arm, which stretched from my wrist to my elbow. I had no fear of such things, being the hardened "Tomboy" that I was. Never had I remembered seeing such an amazing bright blue creature in real life. Most familiar with a land of no trees and very low-to-the-ground plants, the wonders of trees and such lush foliage had me transfixed. It was hot, too. I needed no coat. Even summer days at home usually required a warm jacket. I had been away from Barrow several years earlier, but those were vague memories.

Dad's missionary duty schedule for "out-in-the-field" was three years, then a six-month break. Thus, in the summer of 1954, the family headed back to the states on vacation or furlough in "missionary-speak." Family and friends were as excited and relieved to see us all as we were to see them. Seattle was our base of operations. That was where most of our extended family lived and was Mom and Dad's hometown.

We obtained a car (back in the world as I thought of it) and spent the first few weeks traveling around on a true vacation. We went to California to visit family in that area and visited parks and sites of interest along the way. I remember a park where there was a huge statue of Paul Bunyan's Blue Ox, Babe.

Once back in Seattle, Mom and Dad prepared to go on an extended lecture tour across the United States, giving presentations about the missionary work in northern Alaska to many churches along the way. My older sister, Merrily, little sister, Marti, and baby Clayton, born in 1953, went along on the tour. But my nine-year-old brother, Mark, and I stayed in Seattle with an aunt and uncle and cousins so we could go to school. Merrily was taking correspondence schooling.

Hospital

At some point, Mark, my cousins, and I all came down with a bad case of the flu. When everyone else recovered and were able to return to school, my aunt thought I was just taking longer to recover. However, she became alarmed when she caught Mark carrying me out to the sandbox one day to play with the other kids after school and realized I was feeling better, but just couldn't walk. I was rushed to the doctor. My left leg and right arm were paralyzed, plus other less noticeable symptoms. I was diagnosed with polio!

Mom and Dad were contacted, and they drove day and night to get back to Seattle to be with their sick daughter. The irony of the situation was that Mom and Dad had faced criticism for taking their children to the far north for fear we would contract some disease like tuberculosis or suffer somehow from the cold. But, no, we were healthy as could be while living far from traditional civilization, yet here their little girl caught the dreaded polio virus while on vacation down in the heart of civilization!

I was in the children's hospital in downtown Seattle for about three months. I was six when I got polio. I can't remember too much except a room with at least two other children in beds with railings on them. I was envious of the child in the bed next to the window because she could look out at the world. I would ask a nurse to carry me over to the window so I could look down on the street way below to see if I could see my parents' car parked down there.

It was days before my parents finally reached Seattle from Oklahoma, where they were located when they received word of my illness. My mother said she was crying hard when they finally reached my bedside and I stoically and calmly said that I had been waiting and waiting for them to come. Later, my parents told me that they were so proud of me because all the doctors and nurses had told them that I was the best and most cooperative patient they had ever had.

I was so much more fortunate than many polio victims, because I never suffered breathing problems or had to endure a lung machine. I did spend many weeks in the hospital and went through all the prescribed therapy for regaining use of my limbs. There were water exercises and exercises while lying in bed. Lifting my left leg an inch off the bed brought sweat droplets to my brow. Mom was with me so much of the time. I look back on those days with guilt knowing now what Mother sacrificed to be with me so much and how much of her time I must have stolen from other family members.

When I was able to leave the hospital, Mom and Dad rented a movable hospital bed for me and put it right in my grandmother's living room, where we were living until we could all go home to Alaska. Since I still had to spend so much time in bed during those days, being in the living room kept me connected with the rest of the family. Dad had to return to Barrow in December, but I still needed therapy, so the rest of the family stayed in Seattle for about six more weeks until I was cleared to leave in late January 1955.

I had to be taught how to walk again. Even when I could have limped along, I had been held back from using my right leg until my left leg had built up enough strength through therapy to hold my weight and take steps. I was still growing, and use of the strong leg would accelerate its bone growth and leave the weaker left leg even further behind. When the doctors felt I was ready, I was taught how to walk using support bars and much encouragement. With my fierce determination, mingled with lots of painful tears, I slowly learned to use my legs again.

Once out of the hospital, I needed further therapy. Mom was only five feet tall and weighed about one hundred pounds, yet every day she would carry me uphill many blocks from my grandmother's house to the bus stop to take me to the clinic for the therapy sessions. When I could finally walk again, we were allowed to go home to Alaska, but my mother kept me on a strict exercise regimen so I would continue to gain strength in my stricken limbs. It was months of hard work. Mom would cry right along with me as we struggled through painful exercises.

Keeping up with the other kids at play was hard. Until my legs strengthened, my brother, Mark, often pulled me on a small sled Dad made for me so I could join in activities.

Gradually I became strong again, but never could run well due to the weaker left leg and balance problems. When I stopped growing, my left leg was over five eighths of an inch shorter than the right, and my left foot was a size and a half smaller than my right. Over half the nerve supply to the left leg had been destroyed and what was left had to take on the job for the whole leg, so it would always remain considerably weaker than my "good" leg. But I learned to compensate, and with my strong right leg and a built-up left shoe, I could walk with nary a limp (until I got tired.) My right arm had recovered to normal strength and within a few years most people didn't even know I had any problems at all.

Most polio survivors developed super-achiever character-istics ("A" personalities) and, like so many polio victims, I pushed myself to the limit of my endurance in about everything I did. I went on to excel in most sports, especially if they used mostly upper body strength. During President Kennedy's National Fitness Tests in the 1960s, I scored top in every test except racing. I even tested by using mostly "boy" scoring, which was more difficult than the girls' level of testing.

Leaving Barrow

In 1958, my family regrettably left Barrow. My parents loved northern Alaska and all the wonderful Iñupiat people. However, the Presbyterian Board of National Missions had a policy of not wanting to send missionary children out to school, away from their families. This was unlike the Board of Foreign Missions, where children did get sent away to school. Our family was up to six children by then, three more arriving during the years in Barrow, and the local school only went up to eighth grade back then. My older sister, Merrily, was already leaving home for boarding school. My brother, Mark, and I would soon have to go "out" to school, too. Thus, leaving the Barrow mission field became mandatory.

Before I understood why we had left Alaska, I was somewhat angry with my parents for taking me away from my beloved Arctic world. Sometimes I would curl up in a corner with my old fur parka and hold it just to smell the memories.

Dad accepted a new church position in the town of Sequim, Washington. For four years we lived in this rural community, where I completed eighth grade and began ninth grade. Dad moved on to a church in Seattle after that, and I graduated from Glacier High School there in Seattle in 1967.

Wartes family ready for church Christmas 1957. Left to right, brother Mark, Dad Bill, Clayton, Teena, Marti, Mom Bonnie, older sister Merrily with baby Eldon on her back under her parka.

Return Visit

A highlight for me between my junior and senior year of high school was a trip back to Barrow for the summer. My married sister, Merrily, was living there at the time since my brother-in-law had taken a social service job there. Additionally, Merrily knew the Iñupiaq language well enough to help translate at the new courthouse.

Merrily was expecting her second Barrow-born baby and I went to help out. I was so delighted to be back HOME in Alaska! I spent many an hour hanging out with dear Iñupiat friends and often carried my two-year-old niece on my back under my parka, Iñupiat-style. I was back in my beloved land and blended right in with all my parka-clad friends.

My girlfriend Doreen and I had a hearty laugh one day while walking around town when a tourist came up to me and wanted to take a picture of me with "my" baby on my back inside my parka. After snapping the picture, the tourist gave the baby a closer look and commented, "Oh, she has blue eyes; her daddy must be a white man." My eyes are brown,

Teena and her Wartes family prior to leaving Barrow in 1958, L-R: Rev. Bill Wartes, Merrily, Marti, Bonnie, Teena, Mark, Clayton, baby Eldon on Merrily's back inside parka. The Mission plane is in back. Bowhead whalebone church sign on right."

Teena returned to Barrow in 1965 and often carried her niece Joli on her back Iñupiat-style on her walks around town.

and my light brown hair was tucked inside a hat. After she walked away, Doreen and I cracked up laughing. I was proud to be taken for Iñupiat like my friend.

During my first year at Whitworth College in Spokane, Washington, my family moved to upper-state Michigan, where my dad ministered to four different small church communities. Although I visited my family several times in Michigan, I never lived there and was pretty much out on my own by then.

Meeting Helmericks Family and Jim

During our early family years in Alaska, my dad got acquainted with the Helmericks family living out in the Colville River Delta. Dad had been instructed early on to look up Bud Helmericks to get Arctic survival training and tips on flying in northern Alaska. Bud had many years of Alaskan wilderness experience, had traveled the arctic regions by dogsled and canoe, but had recently upgraded to air transportation so he had valuable experience to pass on to my dad. My dad and Bud both flew a Cessna 170. The two pilots enjoyed flying together on occasion, and my family enjoyed Bud's visits to Barrow.

Jim as a ten year old learning to love the Arctic life.

The Helmericks family and mine soon became dear friends. My older brother and sister and I got to stay with the Helmericks on the Colville for visits several different summers. Bud and Martha's son, Jim, was between Merrily and Mark in age. He occasionally came to visit with us in Barrow.

Jim was staying with my family in Barrow on my tenth birthday when he shot a Snow Goose out behind the village for my birthday dinner. I still have the picture of us standing on our back porch that day, Jim proudly holding up the goose.

After my family moved to Washington State, Jim came and lived several different winters with us to attend public school in order to give his mom a break from correspondence schooling. Later my family cared for Jim's two younger brothers for short periods of time when Bud and Martha went on world

Jim provides dinner for Teena's tenth birthday, Barrow 1958. Teena's mother and little sister Marti in the background.

tours in conjunction with conservation research that Bud was conducting. Our families remained close.

Jim was just like another sibling in my childhood. But during my early college days when Jim was in the Army and sent to Vietnam, our relationship began changing as we wrote letters back and forth daily. Later, after he was out of the Army and we were both visiting my family over Christmas in Michigan, Jim and I became engaged to be married. My brother Mark teased me that I couldn't marry my brother!

Jim wanted to marry then and there, no waiting, but I had promised my parents that I would finish college. Plus, we needed to plan a wedding and coordinate details between family members who lived thousands of miles apart. Jim drove me back to college in Spokane after Christmas break and then returned home to the Arctic to await our wedding day. I finished my junior year of college while getting everything set for an early June wedding in Seattle. We picked a mid-way point for family to converge from two different directions. My family flew out from Michigan and Jim's family came down from Alaska. There were many dear friends and family living in the Seattle area, so we had a large attendance at the wedding.

When the wedding hurdle was over, I was overjoyed to be headed back HOME to Alaska. I had always considered the 1960s to be the period of time when I was simply "Out to school in the Lower 48."

Back to Alaska, My True Home

All the Helmericks headed home to northern Alaska the day after our Seattle-based wedding. Jim and I would be honeymooning in the wilderness of the Brooks Range, and Jim's folks were scheduled to pick up a newly purchased plane before starting the summer's work.

Several days later, Jim and I were settled into the log cabin hidden away on Takahula Lake in the Brooks Range, my first home as a married woman. Takahula had been Jim's first home in the Arctic as well, as he spent several winters there as a young boy. Bud and his first wife, Connie, had built the two-room cabin in the late 1940s. Later, Jim and his mother,

Martha, came to live there with Bud, and this is where Jim began learning about fur trapping, Arctic survival, and many necessary skills that became a firm part of his Alaskan life.

We had been flown into Takahula Lake in a floatplane from Fairbanks, a two-hour flight across one hundred and fifty miles of tundra, spruce forests, hills, and mountains. We passed over the mighty Yukon River and entered the southern edge of the Brooks Range, the large mountain range that bisects interior Alaska and the North Slope.

Takahula Lake is a small lake lying just west of the Alatna River. The closest community was Bettles, thirty miles to the southeast. The lake is in a beautiful spot surrounded by high hills and mountains, and our cabin was the only structure for many miles in all directions. When the floatplane pilot took off, we were a couple truly alone in the wilderness. Back in those days, we had no radios, phones, or any other means of communication with the outside world. We simply had each other and the confidence that we could take care of ourselves and live comfortably in this cozy cabin in the great land that we both loved.

Jim and Teena were married at the South Park Presbyterian Church in Seattle in 1970.

The Takahula cabin was a perfect fit, as if built just for me. I loved it.

The cabin had a full covered porch in front and two rooms front and back. Large windows looked out in three direc-tions. We had to open shutters and remove the nail-board that keeps

Honeymoon on beautiful Takahula Lake in the Brooks Range 1970.

unwanted four-legged guests out in order to enter ourselves. A nail-board is a wide plank with large nails pounded through the board every inch or so and sticking out the other side of the board. It is laid in front of the door with the sharp-pointed nail side up.

The cabin inside was well laid out with a kitchen with shelves, counter and sink, wood cook stove, and a built-in table with benches that looked out over a spectacular view of the lake. The small kitchen had a low counter and with shelves above holding cooking supplies. It was perfect for my short (4'11") stature. Doorways were low to conserve heat, and I didn't even need to duck down to pass through as did most other adults. A built-in platform bed, with a storage area beneath, occupied one corner.

The back room had a stone fireplace taking up nearly the whole back wall, another platform bed, a desk and shelves full of books, another table, and many other items to make for a comfortable life. The cabin and furniture had all been made from local logs and hand tools. We settled in and would see no other people until Jim's parents flew in with their new Cessna 180 floatplane to pick us up several weeks later.

Although this was all familiar for Jim, it was my first time to the area. I was enthralled with the wee cabin, seemingly made just for my small stature, plus was eager to explore the entire area around the lake and cabin.

We spent the next few weeks tramping through the woods and along game trails, climbing the mountain sides, watching the wildlife, and enjoying the peaceful wilderness all around.

There were trails around the lake, the flats at the south end of the lake, Spirit Mountain to the west, Takahula Mountain to the east, which separated the lake from the Alatna River, and Jimmy Lake to the north, high up in a small hollow several miles above the cabin. I had dreamed for many years of coming home to Alaska and I couldn't have been happier.

Inside the cabin was everything needed for a comfortable life. The kitchen was fully equipped with dishes, pans, and utensils. Food and supplies were plentiful. Extra goods had previously been stored in the cabin, so with the small amount of supplies we brought with us, we had everything we needed. I learned to cook on the wood stove, including baking bread and sweets in the small oven. Firewood was plentiful. We hauled our water in a bucket up from the lake, carrying it up the log-supported dirt steps from the shore to the cabin porch, a rise of about fifteen feet. We used an outhouse about twenty feet back in the trees behind the cabin. The sink had a drain that emptied into a bucket to be dumped outside when full. If we felt like taking a bath, a galvanized horse trough tub was available. We lacked nothing.

I fished with a rod and reel for the first time and got so excited catching fish left and right along the shore just below the cabin, that Jim finally suggested I'd better start throwing the live fish back, because we couldn't eat that many before they spoiled. As it was, we ate a lot of fish: trout, pike, round whitefish, and grayling.

Teena hiking around Takahula Lake in 1970.

Walker Lake is eighty miles west of Takahula Lake in the Brooks Range.

We had a canoe, plus a tiny kayak that Jim's father had made, that again seemed to be made just for my small size. I paddled it all around the lake. Our days were full. We had quiet evenings with a good book under a kerosene lamp, and a comfy bed under a soft down quilt. It was a perfect paradise for newlyweds who loved wilderness.

The only damper to our honeymoon was that we both came down with colds given to us by someone in the wedding's greeting line, plus Jim had to deal with a toothache part of the time. However, the days flew by with great joy and contentment.

We were expecting Jim's folks to fly in with their floatplane, *The Helmericks*, the newly-bought Cessna 180, to pick us up about two weeks after arriving at Takahula. However, the days slipped by past the prearranged date. We wondered what the delay was but had no way of finding out. To calm our worries, we kept busy and decided to rebuild the worn steps up to the cabin from the lake's edge. That meant cutting new log pieces for each step and repacking the dirt behind each piece.

Finally one afternoon, a shiny black, white, and gray floatplane circled us, landed on the lake and taxied up to the beach below the cabin. Out jumped Bud and Martha, Jim's folks. Delays were quickly explained as we packed up our gear and closed up the cabin. We were soon off to new adventures as we flew eighty miles west over the mountains to Walker Lake, a twenty-mile-long jewel tucked between mountains on all sides. Bud and Martha had built a new cabin on an island in this lake

Caribou and beautiful scenery at Walker Lake.

several years after Jim and his mother first came to Alaska. By the time I joined the family, Swan Island boasted a main two-room cabin similar to the one at Takahula, but considerably larger, a small guest cabin with storage room attached on the back, a warehouse, a small meat-house, clothesline, and stone walkways between buildings. Another spot on the east side of the lake had a stone-based cabin, and the hillside above was a favorite berry picking site. Later this site was developed further into a commercial wilderness lodge site.

Jim and I occupied the guest cabin while we stayed at Walker Lake for two weeks and helped with guiding clients on the best fishing adventure a person could have. We had a film crew there that year too, as a documentary film was being made about the Helmericks Family and hunting during four seasons in the Arctic. *Edge of the Arctic Ice* would later premier in Minneapolis, Minnesota, in the spring of 1971.

PART TWO

Helmericks Colville Homesite—1970s Onward

Aerial of Anachlik Island looking west. The new house and lodge is on the isthmus between the lake and river.

Chapter 2
Life on the Colville River Delta

How It Began

Let me give more details or history of the family homesite on Anachlik Island. Why here? Well, back in the early 1950s, Jim's parents, Bud and Martha Helmericks chose this island to begin carving out a new home. The vast and intriguing Arctic lands had captured Bud's heart during his earlier years of exploration along the shores of the Arctic Ocean, especially the beauty and diversity of the Colville River, which is Alaska's third largest river stretching three hundred and seventy miles long and draining 20,920 square miles of the great prairie land sloping down between the Brooks Mountain Range and the Arctic Ocean. This led to the Helmericks ownership of one

Living in tents inside snow-houses during the first few winters on Anachlik Island. All you can see are stovepipes sticking out of the snow after a big storm. Jim's dad is in the picture.

hundred sixty acres on Anachlik Island on the eastern face of the Colville River Delta.

It was originally filed as a Homestead but later changed to two adjacent Trade and Manufacturing Sites, all filed on federal land before statehood. Trade and Manufacturing Sites were similar to homesteads but comprised half the land and required the operation of a business on site. Our commercial fishing operations easily qualified. Much of the acres encompasses a large lake which spans the width of the island at its widest stretch. The island is approximately five miles long by two miles wide at its widest and sits on the west side of the most eastern navigable channel of the Colville River Delta.

This island had been totally barren of any human structures or signs of previous usage prior to Bud choosing this site on which to settle, although several old Iñupiat camp sites were located on an island to the east of our island. Eventually the term "homestead" for Helmericks Colville homesite became common just for ease of using a term most people understand.

For the first few years that Jim and his folks used the island, they lived in tents surrounded by snow blocks. The primary reasons for selecting this location was the proximity of the best winter fishing nearby on the East Channel, and the large

One of the earliest cargo flights that landed on the Colville River on the first runway plowed out on the river ice by the tracked tractor that was brought overland from Barrow. The tractor assisted unloading.

Jim and dogs by first house on Anachlik Island built in early 1950s from many loads of materials delivered by a cargo plane. Tall post holds the antenna for the aircraft radio used to guide the aircraft across the northern regions.

freshwater lake which supplied all our water needs year-round and gave a safe landing spot for our floatplanes in summer.

In 1957, the first modern home was constructed from materials flown in aboard thirteen air-cargo flights. Previously, a small track tractor had been purchased and shipped north on a cargo vessel to Barrow and then driven overland the one hundred and sixty-five miles to the Colville to use for construction projects, including a runway on the frozen river ice. By plowing the snow off the ice, a long, smooth surface was made to accommodate the C-46 twin engine cargo plane flown north from Fairbanks. Not only did this first cargo flight backhaul hundreds of pounds of fresh-frozen fish to markets in Fairbanks, but it started a tradition of yearly supply flights that arrived at the close of the winter fishing season full of groceries, fuel, and other needed supplies, then backhauled fish to market.

This first main structure was a two-story frame house built with double outside walls totaling a thickness of ten inches. It took several years to finish, using mostly just hand tools, plus the construction work was only seasonal since other activities took place in several other locations during the year which took the family away to the Walker Lake home in the Brooks Range or elsewhere.

Over the years since that first building, many other buildings have been constructed, including hangers, warehouses, a barn, shops, and several more homes, all adding to the extensive family complex.

Helmericks Homesite (Colville Village) by 1990s.

While the Colville Helmericks Homesite continued its early development in the 1960s, I lived with my family in Washington State and eventually finished my formal schooling through high school and three years of college. I finished college, partly by correspondence and received my BA degree the year after Jim and I were married. Meanwhile, Jim finished his formal schooling through two years at the University of Alaska Fairbanks, bought and learned to fly his own airplane, worked with his Dad in the guiding and fishing businesses, and spent two years in the US Army. During these years, Jim also added his own house to the complex, which I helped finish after we wed, and it became our primary home on Anachlik Island for eighteen years.

My brother Mark Wartes was care-taking the Helmericks Compound on Anachlik Island during part of 1970 while Jim and I were away for our wedding, further college, and flight training. After finishing his service in the US Air Force, Mark returned to the Arctic with Jim in the spring of 1970. Mark took care of the homesite while the Helmericks family was away and soon made the Colville his home, too. Later, he married a girl from Detour, Michigan, Denise Cross, and brought her to live at the Colville. Both their children, Marwan and Marita, were born during their years on the Colville.

Return to the Homesite in 1970

After time at the Walker Lake family home, our thoughts turned to the Arctic Coast where we would soon be heading. Over the years, our homesite on Anachlik Island has been referred to by different names: Helmericks, Helmericks Homestead, Colville Village, and The Colville. It was here that both summer and winter commercial fishing was started to provide the bounty of the Colville River to people throughout Alaska. Jim had already been running the summer fishing operation for a number of years, and we needed to get to the coast to begin that year's operation. I was eager to learn the ropes.

When late June arrived, Jim's dad flew us north to the Arctic coast from Walker Lake so we could get the summer commercial fishing started. With all the extra activities this

There were only three main buildings at the Helmericks Homesite when Teena and Jim arrived in 1970.

early summer held, Jim was late getting the summer fishing underway. First, we went to my new home on Anachlik Island on the east side of the Colville River Delta, the location of the family homesite. We had the beginnings of a modern home next door to Jim's folks' Colville home. Jim had been building on it for several years. It was a two-story frame house, with a three-room apartment and a large storage room on the first floor and our main living quarters on the second floor, with a large kitchen and living room area, two bedrooms and a bathroom. There wasn't much in the upstairs yet, as Jim had been living in the downstairs apartment while he worked on the upstairs. The bedrooms and bathroom were just empty shells and we started with only a few chairs, a single bed, and a small kitchen area in the main room, which also had a barrel wood stove for heat. The kitchen had a small propane cook stove and a few gas-box crates for cupboards. Jim had already outfitted the kitchen with a beautiful set of China dishes, silverware, a nice set of pans, and everything else we needed for housekeeping. However, I barely had time to get acquainted with this home before we moved on.

Summer Commercial Fishing, Niglik

Jim needed to get to work with the commercial fishing business he ran on the west side of the delta during the summer. Nets were set in the furthest west Colville River

Our summer home on the west side of the Colville River Delta where we operated our summer fishing – a tiny black and white striped cabin with Nannie Woods' house in background.

channel to catch the runs of large broad whitefish, which we called Anachlik in Iñupiaq.

Jim's Piper Super Cub, the *Golden Plover*, had been waiting at our main Colville homesite where he had left her before traveling south for the wedding. Taking a few supplies, we flew twenty miles west across the face of the delta and landed on a sandbar just north of the fish camp. There the plane was tied down and we began to open up and move into another small cabin that Bud had built in the early 1950s. This was a one-room structure with attached covered porch. It was compact, with a built-in table, bunk beds, heating stove, cook stove, cupboards, sink, and counter. It even had a tiny toilet room built into the porch and an elevated water-tank for gravity-feed running water to the kitchen sink on the other side of the wall. Again, I felt so comfortable in this tiny house with all the comforts of home. I had actually visited this cabin as a little girl when my dad had brought my brother and me along for a visit to the Helmericks in mid-1950s.

My mother-in-law likes to tell the story of one incident that happened on that particular visit. I was in the cabin by myself at some point and was curious about what was in a shelf I wasn't tall enough to see into. So, I stood up on a travel case sitting on the floor to get higher and unknowingly cracked the mirror inside the case's lid in the process. Jim's mother continued using that case for many years and told people, "Little did I know that that little girl who broke my mirror would become my daughter-in-law!"

Our Niglik cabin and the warehouse Jim built in 1968 for fish processing.

After Jim and I settled into the cabin, getting the nets set out in the river was next on the agenda. Nets were stored in the warehouse Jim had built several years previously. The small boat and engine were also there. All the equipment had to be made ready. I learned how to rig the nets with spreader boards, bridle lines, anchors, and a marker buoy.

I watched and learned how and where to set the nets as Jim got all the nets deployed. He had the process down to a fine-tuned science, knowing exactly where and on which side of the river to set nets in order to catch the most fish, depending on timing for the fish run. He had been running the summer fishing operation on his own since he was thirteen years old.

Jim kept busy with other jobs I couldn't do. After setting nets, I became the main net handler. Jim taught me how to run our fifteen-foot boat, a square-stern Grumman Sportsman canoe, with an eight hp engine. It was important to approach a net from downwind at the shore-side end, shutting the engine off and lifting it from the water and then jumping to the front of the boat to quickly grab the net before the wind blew you back out of reach of the net. I learned to untangle (pick) the fish from the nets with practiced speed, and once back at the shore, how to carry them up to the processing table by hand. I could carry four big fish per hand—one finger in each gill slit, usually tails dragging on the ground with the bigger fish.

All the fish were laid out on a large plywood table where we sorted the fish for various processes. Some fish were frozen whole down in our ice cellar, dug deep in the permanently frozen ground, known as permafrost. Jim cut hundreds of eight-to-ten-pound fish for smoking and drying. This Pivsi, as it was called, was a favorite treat with all locals, including us. Jim was an expert Pivsi maker and sold his fish all across northern Alaska. Another special treat Jim prepared was called auruq, which was still being eaten by a few older Iñupiat people. This was soured fish similar to an oriental favorite eaten by the Japanese and Vietnamese. Jim would half fill a large fish sack, plastic-lined burlap potato bag, with whole fresh fish, close the bag and set it in the shade for a day, then put it in our ice cellar. As the clump of fish slowly froze, it soured into auruq. The smell was almost more than I could bear, let alone the thought of eating it! But it is all in what you get used to. If I had eaten it as a child, I would probably have had no qualms eating it.

Besides cutting fish and running the smokehouse, which was a time-intensive job, Jim flew loads of fish over to the much bigger ice cellar at our main homesite for storage, where the fish were laid out on shelves to freeze individually. He would also fly bags of fresh fish to market in Barrow or other villages.

I picked nets once or twice a day, depending on how heavy the fish run was progressing. Sometimes it was too windy, with rough waves, to go out on the river, and then I had to wait for the high wind to go down. There were days when the fog would move in quickly and I would be out picking a net and look up into a stark white world, unable to even see the riverbanks on either side of where I was floating next to a net. Occasionally, I got so disoriented in the fog that I did not know which way to go to get back home. I wasn't that far away most of the time, only a mile or so, but fog could get so dense that you could hardly see your hand in front of your face. I would just start the engine and head out until I could see a bank and follow it along until I recognized home port.

Sometimes I had to go out several times for one full picking of all the nets because the nets were too full to carry all the fish in the boat at one time. We had a large flat box built to fit

Teena in Grumman Sportsman canoe picking Broad Whitefish (Anachlik) from a net set in the west channel of the Colville River 1970.

in the middle of the boat to carry the freshly-caught fish. We never allowed fish to lie in the boat itself. In fact, it was a no-no to even let a fish hang inside the gunwale while working to get it untangled from the net. Fish slime in the boat made it dangerously slippery. I learned to extract a large eight-to-ten-pound fish from the net and throw it into the box without ever letting it touch anywhere inside the boat.

I had to pick the net bare-handed in extremely frigid water. It caused my fingers to swell all the time and Jim had me remove my wedding ring before we started fishing. One summer Jim had learned the importance of this when he had to have a ring sawed off his swollen finger when he forgot to remove it before working in cold water. We stayed at the summer fish camp until mid-July. The last major whitefish run would be over by then.

We had neighbors while at the Niglik, the Iñupiat name for our fish camp area. The family of George and Nannie Woods lived next door in a small house my father-in-law helped build for them in the early 1950s. They were the only Iñupiat family still living in the area full-time that hadn't moved to Barrow for school and amenities. George had passed away several years before I arrived, and Nannie was alone except when her grown children were with her. Nannie was like our Iñupiat grandma, a dear soul who would sit and drink tea with me and visit in her broken English, both of us using a spattering of Iñupiaq. For me, it helped refresh much of the native language I had lost during the years away from Alaska, and I helped Nannie improve her English.

Since George's passing on, Nannie still missed him terribly and she would talk about him, shedding tears, and I would commiserate with her as we visited over a cup of tea. George was buried on a small mound behind Nannie's house.

Nannie helped me with parka patterns and taught me sewing skills that would help me sew fur garments for my family for years to come. I loved watching Nannie scrape the fur off of a dried seal hide, using ash to make the hair slip easily, or sew on a pair of seal-skin mukluks with her fingers whipping out stitches with enviable speed. Nannie shared her native foods with us, and we shared candy treats or other white-man food with her. Her akutuq, or Eskimo ice cream, made from whipped caribou fat with berries mixed in, was a special treat. One of Nannie's favorite foods was fish head soup. Boiling up a big pot of fish heads, she loved to eat the delicious cheek patches and gills. Jim always saved the big Anachlik heads for her when he cut fish for drying.

Big Game Guiding

After summer fishing, we started our big-game hunting season. Jim was a professional Alaskan Registered Guide. He had worked alongside his dad, Harmon (Bud), for many years as a young assistant guide, and obtained his Alaskan Registered Guide's license at twenty-one, one of Alaska's youngest big-game guides. He had already bought his own airplane, spent time in Fairbanks learning to fly it, and got his private pilot's license in 1965. He had been flying and guiding clients for five years before we married in 1970. Later, I obtained an Assistant Guide license.

The guiding season started with walrus hunting out of Barrow. Jim's dad had set up use of a large hunting boat with an Iñupiat crew to travel out to the ice flows north of the village of Barrow to hunt for the massive walrus. A large male walrus would make an exceptional trophy for a client, plus supply

Hunting walrus in Al Hopson's boat offshore of Barrow in July 1970.

tons of meat for the village. Usually, a bearded seal would also be harvested, a trophy hide for the client and more meat for the local people. This hunt usually took many hours of travel among a vast expanse of floating ice, many miles away from the coast. It was only possible when ice conditions allowed vessels to negotiate the broken ice. During some summers, the ice was jammed tight into the beach and boat travel was impossible.

Late July 1970 was the only year I went with Jim to Barrow for this hunt. The US government had passed the Marine Mammal Protection Act of 1972 that protected all sea mammals from hunting by non-natives. This shut down Bud and Jim's guiding and hunting of all seals, walrus, and polar bears. The last sea mammal taken by our family was a ringed seal I shot about one hundred miles offshore on my birthday, June 9, 1972.

I was flown out onto the Arctic pack-ice to shoot my first and only seal. It was a one-shot-kill, leaving only one bullet hole in the hide, since the shot entered through the eye. When hunting seal out on the ice where they haul out of breathing holes to sunbathe, the shot must be an instant kill or the animal flips

Teena and Jim's mother Martha at seal kill, June 1972.

down the hole and is lost. I had the hide tanned and it has been used for a cover on my piano bench ever since.

Sheep Camp

Mid-August brought travel to our big-game hunting camps inland. In August of 1970, I flew with Jim into my first hunting camp to begin the fall guiding season with a Dall sheep hunt high in the Brooks Range. Jim's *Golden Plover* was equipped with large thirty-five-inch tundra tires. Jim could land his plane most anywhere there was a reasonably flat area of three hundred to five hundred feet long which might be a sandbar or field along a river, or a tundra area up high on a mountain. He was already an extremely skilled "bush pilot," as Alaskan pilots who fly mostly in remote areas with no approved airstrips are called.

We set up a base camp in a small valley surrounded by six-to-seven-thousand-foot mountains, the largest one we called Square Shoulders. Jim landed on a short stretch of tundra alongside a small stream that meandered through the narrow valley then rushed on down through a narrow canyon and later fed into the Alatna River, twenty miles downstream. Jim's Dad would bring hunting clients in with his Cessna 180 floatplane and land on a stretch of the Alatna River near a sandbar where Jim could land. There they would transfer people and gear so Jim could fly them into the higher hunting camp. With

Jim sweeping snow off his Golden Plover with willow bush in Sheep Camp, 1971.

Teena and client at Sheep Hunting Basecamp in Brooks Range.

no long-distance means of communication back then, Jim and his dad had to rely on each other's well-laid plans for certain rendezvous times and places. Dad had the bigger, faster plane and Jim had the *Golden Plover* that could go higher into the mountains where the floatplane could not land. They worked as a team.

I became "chief-cook-and-bottle-washer" at base camp, plus kept an eye on the plane as Jim took his clients higher into the mountains on foot, often setting up a little Spike Camp and staying until a sheep was taken.

I kept busy at the base camp. One activity was setting up and checking a trapline daily. The valley was over-run with Arctic ground squirrels, and I trapped over a hundred that first year so I could make myself a fancy women's dress parka. The squirrels needed to be skinned, and then the hides stretched and dried on bent willow branches. Later I sent these hides to be commercially tanned for my sewing projects.

Our valley was just on the edge of the tree line. We actually had to walk down to the lower end of the valley to cut down dead trees for firewood to heat our tent. I would gather more wood for the stove, carry water from the stream, keep the stew-pot simmering, and various other camp chores. There

Teena and baby Derek with grizzly bear.

were grizzly bears meandering through the valley, several families of wolves making their circuit through the valley, Dall sheep dotting the mountain sides, and many small critters throughout the area like the Arctic ground squirrels, locally called parka squirrels, the occasional porcupine, and many species of birds. I loved watching all the animals and had no fear of them. They respected our camp and kept their distance as they continued about their own agenda with little concern, and I went about my daily business.

My third year in Sheep Camp was the exception to all the wildlife wandering through our camp valley being unobtrusive. An old female grizzly began returning to the area frequently and snooping around. This made me nervous, especially with a client's young daughter staying with me and sleeping in a separate tent. With the old sow becoming increasingly bold, I finally decided, after numerous unsuccessful attempts to force her to vacate the area, that it was time to dispatch this unpredictable menace. Early the next morning, still in my nightgown, the deed was done. I had to go back into the tent to retrieve baby Derek, who was awakened by the loud bang, as was the young girl in the nearby tent. I had created more work for myself, but at least life in camp could return to normal.

I would watch the mountainsides and upper valley constantly, waiting to see Jim and client coming back with full packs, and a set of horns tied to the top of the client's pack. Jim carried most of the delicious meat in his pack, and the client usually had the hide and horns.

One day I heard several shots straight up the mountainside from base camp. I got my spotting scope set up and studied the mountain top, finally picking out two tiny figures moving around. I was surprised to see them because it meant they had hiked across several mountain tops to get there, having left camp two days earlier for a more northeastern area.

I kept an eye on their progress and watched them working in the same spot for an hour or more. I wondered what was taking so long! They must have gotten a sheep, or why else were they hanging around the same spot for so long?

Finally, the tiny figures began moving down toward me. I watched them appear larger and larger as they descended, marveling at how straight downhill they were moving. It took several hours. Both men were exhausted when they finally dragged into camp. I had to help Jim lower his pack, which was well over one hundred pounds, off his shoulders. He had a pack full of meat and one set of horns on top. The client had his set of horns and the sheep hides. No wonder it took longer than I had expected for skinning and butchering at the mountaintop. Jim had decided to take a second sheep for extra meat since they were within sight of base camp; however, the steep climb back down the mountainside was an especially difficult hike while packing the meat of two sheep.

Teena's third year in Sheep Camp with diapers to wash.

While the hunters ate and rested, I began caring for the sheep hides. Jim had taught me how to skin out lips and ears on trophy capes and how to remove brain matter from a sheep skull. Fried brains are a delicacy we loved and that was always part of our breakfast after a successful hunt. Heart, liver, and tongue are also delicacies which became part of our early meals after fresh meat arrived in camp.

During my first year in Sheep Camp, we had a full week between clients where Jim and I had free time to explore up and down the mountain ravines that spidered out from our main base-camp valley. It was fun for me to get to hike with Jim and see more of the surrounding countryside. Like his father, Jim had a mile-eating stride, and I was always lagging behind no matter how hard I tried to keep up, so Jim was forever stopping and waiting for me. Besides seeing lots of gorgeous, pristine wilderness, we found treasures like an old, bleached sheep skull with full-curl horns still attached, perhaps an old ram that fell from a high mountain crag, to add to our museum collection.

We discovered the remains of an ancient camp and deducted someone had once come down this valley and stopped to build a raft to get down the creek to the Alatna River and then on further

Teena with baby Derek on her back sitting by the last tree down the valley from Sheep Camp in 1973.

south. We found an old lean-to, evidence of trees being chopped down, a leveled area beside the stream to launch a raft, and a few old tin cans next to a fire-ring. Jim's dad told us later that very few places in the Brooks Range had been left untraversed by gold miners in the early 1900s. Our fantasy that we were the first people to walk this particular valley was crushed.

When unexpected delays or changes in plans cropped up, we would see Dad fly over our camp, and we would run to our plane and turn on the aircraft radio to exchange information: "So and so had been delayed." "Hang tight." "New schedule ...."

One particularly long delay had us fantasizing what we would do to survive a winter if transportation were somehow cut off, how we could shoot enough passing caribou to eat and have hides to cover our tent for extra warmth.

Our cabin on Takahula Lake was about a half hour's flight from our Sheep Camp, and sometimes we spent time there between sheep hunts. In fact, that is where we stored most of our mountain camping gear between seasons. We always stored our prairie-schooner tent inside the cabin, hanging from ropes from the ceiling so the voles wouldn't get at it when no one was around. One year, when Jim and I set it up in Sheep Camp we discovered that voles had managed to climb down the ropes to the tent and made a bed in it for winter. When we unfolded the tent, there were holes here and there all over. I cut the extra door flap off the tent and used that canvas to cut and sew patches. It looked funny, but it gave us back our snug home, instead of a tent full of peep holes that let the cold and wind inside.

Moose and Other Big Game Hunting

With sheep hunting completed, we moved on to a camp north of the mountains along the Anaktuvuk River, mainly to hunt moose. This was a beautiful area of high hills and deep river valleys, with tall willows and small lakes—prime moose habitat. Occasionally, caribou and even a wolf or wolverine could also be found here, animals our hunting clients were allowed to take if they wanted. Our clients would stay with us for two weeks. Our guiding was for quality of experience, not quantity of clients, or game taken.

Clients not only experienced Arctic conditions, landscape and wildlife, but were also taught a lot of survival skills and appreciation for outdoor living. Some clients had permits for and wanted to hunt all available game, others just wanted one or two trophies and mostly the wilderness experience. They got to fly across vast stretches of the Arctic from camps in the Brooks Range to camps along the Anaktuvuk River in the northern foothills to our modern home on the edge of the Arctic Ocean at the face of the Colville River Delta.

We had comfortable camps with tents heated with small wood stoves. I loved camping. Life was simple. Simple meals, easy, quickly completed chores like wood gathering for a small stove, willow branch or goose wing for a broom, plenty of time to enjoy the sounds of nature all around: the tinkling stream, chirping birds, chattering Arctic ground squirrels, howling wolves, the patter of rain on the tent, wind rustling the tent or willow bushes. Even if it was storming, our tent was always well lashed down and a warm, secure shelter.

Although fresh meat was consumed in the camps, most of the meat obtained during the guiding seasons became our family's main meat supply for the year. Meat was butchered and hauled back to our meat-processing building on the Colville from the hunting camps, where it was cut up, made into ground meat and sausage, ham cured, corned, dried, packaged, and stored in our ice cellar where it froze quickly.

Our Golden Plover with skis for operations on ocean ice, offshore from the Colville River Delta.

*C-206 on
wheelskis
on lake ice
for ice/snow
operations.*

Fall Freezeup

It was always a race every fall to finish the guiding and hunting operations before freeze-up forced floatplane operations to end, and hunting camps to close. Once the hunting season was behind us and happy clients headed south, our next concern was getting ready for freeze-up and winter. Our *Golden Plover* remained on her big tires in fall, but other family planes were usually on floats, and were flown to Fairbanks for gear changes, although a few times we were forced to replace floats with wheels or skis here on the Colville homesite. In the earliest days, a giant outdoor tripod was built to lift a plane for gear change, but later, once the big hanger was built, we used a special lift built into the hanger rafters. Depending on spring flying work, our airplanes could also be put on skis for snow and ice operations off-runway.

Winter Commercial Fishing

Once freeze-up is complete and the river ice is thick enough to safely walk on, our winter commercial fishing operation starts. This depends on weather conditions each year, but usually is late September or early October when we start stringing gill nets below the river surface ice to catch fish swimming in the water below the ice. We catch mainly Arctic Cisco, Least Cisco, and Humpback Whitefish as they feed and move about in the delta face for several months each fall.

Jim and his folks had been commercially fishing with nets under the ice since the early 1950s. They held the only commercial fishing licenses on the North Slope for many years.

Jim and Teena pulling the nets and picking fish. Homesite buildings can be seen in the background.

We started by knowing ahead of time where the right depth of water was found in order to set the nets in the best location for the fish runs. The ice needed to be frozen several inches thick in order to support our weight. Nets and equipment were hauled out to the setting site on a small hand-sled to begin with, later a snowmachine and sled was used.

The boys sorting fish by species and counting them for reporting to Alaska Department of Fish and Game.

Sacking frozen whole fish for sending to market throughout Alaska. Clyde is helping Isaac weigh the fish sacks.

Our snowmachine with box for hauling fish off the ice with our house on the left in the distance. The damage to the fish box was done by the polar bear.

Holes about one and a half foot diameter were cut in the ice with a handheld ice chopper (duke) in a straight line about fifteen feet apart. Enough holes must be opened to cover the length of the net to be set. Next, we dropped a weighted line that was connected to a long rope down the first hole. Using a long pole with a hooked end, we reached in under the ice from the second hole to catch the line hanging down from the first hole and pulled it under the ice back to the second hole.

We continued doing this from hole to hole until we had the long rope strung under the ice for one hundred and fifty feet to match the length of the net we intended to set. Once the rope extended under the ice for the entire length necessary, it was attached to the net at the first hole and the net was pulled under the ice, the rope coming up on top again from the last hole. Often several nets were set in a line to make use of the previous net's last hole.

Short ropes attached to the ends of the net were tied to strong sticks we froze into the ice on the edges of the first and last hole. These sticks leaned out at an angle over the holes to hold the ropes in the center of the hole. After a net was set, the holes between the first and last hole were allowed to freeze over and were no longer needed. The net was then stretched out in the water under the ice and small cork floats strung along the top of the net kept it floating upright. A weighted leadline kept the lower end of the net stretched down near the bottom of the river so the net didn't freeze into the underside of the surface ice. Having at least two people to manage the nets and the pull rope was best, as one person could guide the net in or out of the hole as the second person pulled on the net or rope.

As the fishing season progressed, the nets were left in the water under the ice about a day and then pulled back up and picked of fish. Only enough net was pulled out of the water at a time that could be cleaned of the flopping fish before they began to stiffen with the cold. The fish were sorted by species by tossing them to opposite sides of the net, and then they were counted and left to freeze on the ice as the net got pulled back under the ice. This was done daily during the weeks the fish run continued, usually through November.

After all the nets—some years only a few, some years dozens—were cleaned of fish, the frozen fish were gathered into a large box on a snowmachine sled and hauled up to the storage building for later sacking and marketing in eighty-to one-hundred-pound bags. They were packaged as whole fresh-frozen fish and were sold throughout Alaska.

Chapter 3
Family Life

Our Children

Jim and I have four sons, all born during 1972–1981. They were born in Fairbanks with the same doctor delivering them all. I obviously had to leave home for a certain amount of time prior to each delivery as Jim was not interested in

Jim and Teena and three boys in 1979 with first two-story house built on the homesite behind them, which was Bud and Martha's (Jim's parents) home.

Our boys in early 1981: Derek age 9, Jay age 5, Isaac age 3, and Aaron age 9 months.

home-delivery. Depending on circumstances and time of year, this was several months or several weeks. Getting back home as soon as possible was always top priority. Jim was able to be with me for our first baby only. Work and other responsibilities kept him on the Colville for the birth of our other three boys.

All our children benefited from my early Alaskan experiences. I was fortunate to be well acquainted with how to live and work in the far north with a baby to care for. Before our first child was born, Jim had seen to having a larger fur parka made for me that would accommodate a baby. No matter how cold it was when I needed to be outdoors, I could tuck the baby up inside my parka on my back and he would be cozy and warm. A belt around the outside of the parka at waist level held the baby securely in place. I had learned how to carry a baby Iñupiat-style as a young girl in Barrow, plus I carried my nieces on my back many hours when living with my sister in Barrow in 1965.

I would carry my baby on my back even if he was fussy in the house by just tucking him up on my back inside a large shirt or jacket and holding him up with a tie around my waist. One of the benefits of this method is that the weight of the child is evenly spread out across your shoulders. This carry method freed my arms and hands to continue working on whatever needed doing, like cooking or washing dishes. I completed many outdoor chores like milking our goats, collecting chicken eggs, feeding the rabbits, and carrying firewood with a baby on my back.

In the spring of 1972, when I realized I was pregnant, Jim and I flew to Fairbanks so I could get a check-up. I went to the family doctor, Dr. Lawrence Dunlap, who had delivered Jim's younger brothers (as well as all four of our children eventually). All was well and we had to make special financial arrangements since the usual maternity plan, where the mother-to-be had monthly check-ups, would not fit our circumstances. We had no idea when and how my next medical check-up would be. We were given all the usual information at a first check-up. I was able to get one further check-up at the Barrow hospital later that summer. All was still progressing well; baby and I were in good health.

Pregnancy changed few of my daily activities. It was a busy life and about all that was different was slipping in a wee afternoon nap when I could. There were many guests or hunting clients that needed to be fed or dealt with, plus the usual daily chores and housework.

However, I did discover that my pregnancy required some changes in the intensity level of my physical activities. Our fall-time commercial fishing activities were probably the most demanding physically, and I did have to be careful not to over-do the lifting work involved with sacking frozen fish for market.

Derek, Jay, Isaac, and Aaron, 1982.

We would lay out rows and rows of fish on our raised walkways between the buildings, so they froze hard individually before we bagged them up in large, lined burlap bags (later we used large fiber bags). Each bag weighed eighty to one hundred pounds when full. Dressed warmly for the cold, I would stand next to the walk and roll a bag down, begin filling the bag with fish while keeping the fish neatly lying lengthwise in the bag. As the bag filled up, the sides were unrolled until filled nearly to the top, taking about sixty to eighty fish depending on their size. The bag would be standing up and leaning against the walkway. The hardest part was the shaking down of the bag as it was being filled, to help settle the frozen fish more evenly. As the bag got full, you were jockeying about sixty-eighty pounds. This was hard work, especially after handling dozens of bags.

Room was left in the top of the bag, so it could be drawn together and closed. We used heavy string and large needles about six inches long to sew the bags closed, creating ears on each side of the top of the bag to which one could grab a hold of to move the bag around. String precut in the warm house hung around my neck. Threading the needle in the cold with mittens on was always a challenge. This was one job I spent many hours doing, but I did have to go easier during my pregnancies.

Derek's First Trip Home

Several memorable events remain firmly in my mind in connection with Derek's arrival and incorporation into the Helmericks family. That June when I was pregnant with my first baby, I got to hunt my first and only ring seal one hundred miles offshore on the Arctic Ocean icepack. It was the last sea mammal taken by anyone in our family due to the passage of the U.S. Marine Mammal Protection Act of 1972, which allowed Alaska natives to continue hunting them. Another significant event with our first baby was pregnancy complications. Then there was Derek's unique first trip home to our Colville Homesite, a forty-two-hour drive by tractor and sled over the tundra and ocean ice during the dark, cold days of January. These stories actually need to start the fall prior to his arrival.

In early winter of that year while pregnant with Derek, we had our usual cargo plane chartered from Fairbanks to bring annual supplies in, and then to transport our fish to market. This took place in November after fall fishing was complete and the river ice was thick enough to build a long runway. Our tractor was used to push snow aside to create a smooth surface on the ice about twenty feet wide by two thousand feet long. Rows of empty drums with diesel flare pots sitting on top were used to light the runway during the dark.

Supplies had been ordered like groceries, fuel in fifty-five-gallon drums, lumber or any other supplies needed, and delivered to the airlines in Fairbanks, loaded on the cargo C-46 and headed north on the designated day. On the northern end, we had to have the runway and bags of fish ready. When the plane arrived, it was a huge job manually unloading the plane and reloading it several times with many bags of fish. The plane took a load of fish to Barrow to be delivered to Tom Brower's store, Cape Smythe Trading Company. It returned to the Colville to be loaded again for Fairbanks. Much of our year's fuel supplies came back from Barrow, since the fuel had been delivered there by ship in the summer. Heavy equipment could load the plane on the town end, but here at the Colville, we had bush techniques like using a large tire below the cargo door to push full drums out the door and catch the heavy drum when it dropped. Then the drum would be manually rolled out of the way and the next drum dropped. We also used planks to make an improvised ramp from the plane's cargo door down to the ice. Supplies or equipment were carefully slid down this ramp.

Loading the fish bags aboard the plane was just plain, exhausting grunt labor. We had a few fellows hired to help, and we were proud of the speed at which we could unload and reload a large plane like that. Time was critical. The outboard engine was left idling, so start-up in the cold was not a problem. After the plane left, all the supplies had to be moved up on the island and put away.

That November of 1972, this usual process was a bit different in that many of the cases of groceries arriving had to be put up in our house before the plane left, since Jim and I boarded and traveled to Fairbanks aboard that cargo plane. It was a hectic few hours of intense work. I remember Jim being drenched with sweat from all the heavy labor of moving so much freight and heavy fish bags. We were miserably cold due to exhaustion and Jim's wet clothing as we rode south on jump seats inside the cold cargo compartment.

The next day in Fairbanks, I had a doctor's appointment to check on my pregnancy which was now in the seventh month. The doctor was quite upset with me, since my extremely active lifestyle and all the hard work in the preceding days had pushed me into the possibility of early labor. The baby was already dropped into birth position and things were happening to threaten a premature birth. I was put on medication to delay the start of labor and told to take it easy. That gave the baby another month.

We were staying with Jim's folks, who had moved to Fairbanks for the winter months to put Jim's younger brothers, Mark and Jeff, in public school. My brother, Mark, and sister-in-law Denise were still back on the Colville enjoying a quiet mid-winter by themselves and taking care of everything there.

Christmas came and went, and we still had nearly a month to wait for the birth of our baby, but Derek James decided to arrive two days after Christmas. Labor was quick (I can't say easy) since he was practically ready to fall out by then. He was a respectable six pounds, two ounces, but dropped below six pounds in the first few days. However, he quickly gained weight and both mom and baby did well.

Jim and I were anxious to get home to the Colville. A new, larger tractor was purchased. Two large sleds, twenty and thirty feet long, were being built for the John Deere 350 crawler to pull. These preparations ended up delaying our departure for home by over a month. Arrangements were made to fly the tractor, sleds, plus many other supplies up to Prudhoe Bay in a large cargo plane. It would land on the runway servicing the new Prudhoe Bay Oil Field, called Deadhorse Airport. We would then have to drive the assembled "cat-train" overland about eighty miles west to reach the Colville.

The day finally arrived when all was ready. The tractor, sleds, and supplies were transported on the cargo aircraft. Jim, I, baby Derek, and two other fellows making the journey with us flew to Prudhoe Bay on the regularly scheduled airline passenger plane.

I waited inside the Deadhorse terminal caring for my five-week-old baby while Jim, Roy Nieman and Elliot Larson assembled the tractor, sleds, and supplies for our journey. Building supplies were sorted through and a few sheets of plywood were extracted and tacked together into a makeshift shelter on the thirty-foot sled. It was simply an eight-by-eight-by-four-foot structure just big enough to supply shelter for a few people and supplies necessary for the journey. All supplies were loaded on both sleds, including drums of fuel for the tractor, a new snowmachine, a basket dogsled, and two sled-dogs bought in Fairbanks.

It took the fellows three and a half hours to finish loading the sleds and getting all ready to depart. Jim came to the terminal to get Derek and me and helped tuck us into a corner of the plywood shack. We were bundled in down sleeping bags, and I was wearing my heavy Iñupiat-style fur parka. The baby was held comfortably in one arm inside my parka. We couldn't stand up inside, but at least it provided some shelter from the cold winter weather. We had only a two-burner camp stove for heat, which doubled for cooking. Still, it was rarely above freezing in the shack.

Heads turned in puzzlement as our cat-train headed out at 4 p.m. on February 9, 1973 from the airline's yard and started our trek home. Those watching us leave were all oil-field-related people only on the North Slope for the work. I'm sure they shook their heads in amazement as these people, even with a tiny baby, headed out into the wilds of the Arctic night. The temperature was minus ten degrees Fahrenheit when we first departed but dropped down to minus thirty-five degrees Fahrenheit later that night and remained in the minus thirties for the rest of the trip. The camp stove barely kept the inside of the shelter above freezing. In fact, our pot of water would

Our "cat-train" crossed many miles of tundra and ocean ice to get to our home on the Colville River Delta.

freeze if set off the stove. Our two little Lhasa Apso house dogs stayed curled up on a sleeping bag to stay warm.

We followed the oil industry's gravel roads out of the oil field area, heading north-westward. When the roads ended, we headed north to the Arctic Ocean shoreline near Beechey Point in order to follow the coastline around into Harrison Bay and then on into the Colville River Delta.

As I sat inside the plywood shack, I had the impression of riding in a loud, bumpy train traveling at thirty to forty miles an hour. In reality, we were moving a barely two miles per hour or even less in extremely rough areas. Jim could walk along at his normal pace and get ahead of the tractor.

We stopped only long enough to eat and fuel the tractor. Roy Neiman and Elliot Larson would come squat inside the shelter and eat warm meals Jim prepared, then go pump fuel into the tractor's fuel tank with a hand pump. The drums of fuel sat at the front of the first sled. Then off we'd go again. Navigation was by dead reckoning and Jim's knowledge of the terrain, mostly visible only in moonlight. The sun was up only a few hours a day in February.

I mostly stayed in my corner of the shack, only responsible for the baby. Feeding him was no problem as I was nursing him, and this was easily done inside my roomy parka.

Diaper changing times were a bit more complicated, since it had to be quickly done outside the parka. Jim would help by holding a flashlight up for me and I would work as fast as I could. We had planned to have a nice kerosene lantern to use, however we made the mistake of buying a new lantern and not checking to make sure it worked. When we went to light it for the first time, we discovered it was missing the wick!

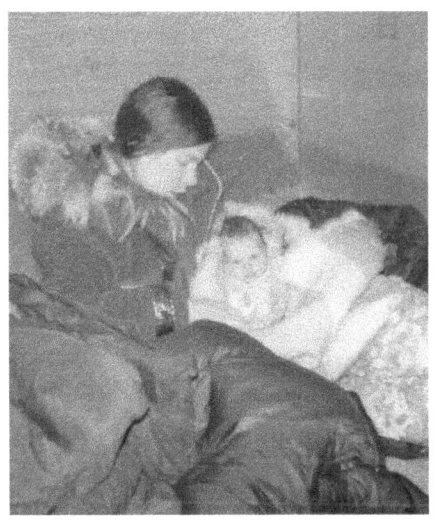

Teena cares for baby Derek inside shack on tractor sled.

Consequently, our only light inside the shack was the burner flame from the small stove or flashlights.

We traveled all Friday and into Saturday, with Elliot and Roy trading off driving and sleeping. Jim cared for me and the dogs, kept the stove fueled and running, fixed meals, got snow to melt for drinks, and performed various other chores. Occasionally the sled would suddenly lurch to a stop, throwing everyone forward. Jim would get out and go check on what was going on. Usually, it was some obstruction that had loomed up in front of the tractor's lights which would have to be circumvented—a large snowdrift or a crevice in the ice.

We reached the DEW Line site at Oliktok at 3 a.m. Sunday morning and stopped for coffee and a visit with friends working at this Distant Early Warning military site. These were our closest neighbors from home, now only fourteen miles on down the coast into the Colville River Delta. I was stiff from my cramped ride and the bright lights inside the buildings hurt my eyes after hours in near darkness. But it was good to be up and about. Of course, seeing a baby was a real treat for all the folks working there.

It wasn't long after getting underway again before our buildings became visible on the distant horizon. Our excitement mounted quickly, for we had been gone from home for two months. I couldn't help but want to stand out on the front of the sled watching our home draw nearer, although it was still seven hours before we pulled up in the yard at 11 a.m. Sunday morning, forty-two hours after leaving Deadhorse Airport.

There was only one building in the Colville home complex showing smoke escaping from the chimney, our two-story house, occupied only in its small downstairs apartment. As we drove up, Mark and Denise Wartes, my brother and sister-in-law, rushed out to greet us. Over the past eight weeks, they had held down the fort and had seen no one since the day we left in November. Our arrival was expected, but there was no way to know exactly when it would be due to no phones or radio communications back then. As people converged, there was a lot of excited commotion with barking dogs, happy chatter and new introductions. This long trek across the white frozen prairie and ice-shrouded ocean and river was quite a unique trip home for tiny Derek.

Since our lifestyle changed little with the birth of Derek, I was able to continue going with Jim to various locations away from our main homesite on Anachlik Island. We would pack up what we could fit in the *Golden Plover* and fly off to our Niglik Fish Camp on the western side of the delta or hunting camps we used in the fall hunting season. We knew how to live on sparse supplies: a small assortment of food that would supplement wild game we could get along the way, a few changes of clothes, survival gear always in the plane which included a small tent and sleeping bags, and now a few extra diapers for the baby. Since I breastfed the baby, no extra milk or paraphernalia was needed. Plus, I always had my parka or a light jacket, depending on weather, in which to carry the baby and continue with all the camp chores, my other duties, or even go for long hikes with my baby secure on my back. To this day, I still think this is the easiest and most comfortable way to carry a baby, despite all the new baby-packing devices now on the market for parents.

More Children

Our second son, Jay Gregory, was a spring baby and arrived while the extended family was busy working on a big Union Oil Company exploratory project just offshore of the Colville River Delta. That story was covered in an article I wrote for Alaska Magazine in 1977. I was a busy mother with

Teena carries Derek inside her parka.

a newborn baby, a three-and-a-half-year-old, the usual home duties, farm chores, guests, and my work involving support of the Union Oil project. I ran the multiple radios that coordinated the work between ground vehicles, incoming and outgoing aircraft, and the various contractors.

One day, I shocked everyone across that radio network with an exasperated plea, "PLEASE give me just a few minutes break, so I can sit down and nurse the baby!" There was amazing radio silence for fifteen minutes or so. That was quite a comment going out over the airwaves, considering it was on the edge of the Arctic Ocean and those listening were hardened oil field workers not used to hearing anything family-related on the job.

One day in May, when Jay was less than two months old, Jim, Derek, and I with baby Jay under my parka on my back headed out by snowmachine to visit friends and have Sunday dinner at the military-operated DEW Line site, nearly fourteen miles northeast of our home in the Colville River Delta.

It was well below zero, but there was beautiful sunshine and long days by that time of year. We had our warm parkas and gear, so it was a wonderful drive and the folks working at the DEW Line were delighted to see us, especially the kids. They usually served long hitches and missed their families.

I think most mothers would be horrified at the thought of taking a tiny baby out in the freezing cold like that, but I was used to this and confident in the ability to keep my baby warm and comfortable inside my fur parka where he was cuddled securely next to my own body warmth.

Our third son, Isaac James, was a fall-time baby. Jay was barely two and Derek was six by then. I went to town to deliver him and high-tailed it back home as soon as I could. Jim was busy flying almost every day on air taxi business, guiding and caring for hunting clients, and managing the family and all the duties at home while I was gone—quite a feat! I told Jim it would be a lot easier if I just had the baby at home, but he would have nothing to do with that. When I flew north from Fairbanks on a commercial jet just three days after Isaac's birth, Jim had to fly our Cessna 206 on floats to a lake near the Deadhorse Airport in Prudhoe Bay to pick us up. The only commercial flight into Deadhorse at the time was an evening flight, so by the time Jim picked us up and we returned to our home lake by our house, it was dark. The only lights were from our house windows. Those lights and a slight shimmer of moonlight on the lake's surface guided Jim in.

Our fourth son, Aaron Woodrow, was another mid-winter baby like Derek. My mother came from Washington State to meet me in Fairbanks prior to his birth and then stayed with us at our Colville homesite until after Christmas. After the brief Fairbanks stay and Aaron's arrival, we were able to fly commercially to Deadhorse again, but this time our planes were hangered for the dark, cold days of winter and we had to drive the seventy-five miles home by pickup truck over gravel roads and then on a trail over the ocean ice into the Colville River Delta.

With our first child, I followed the book when it came to introducing solid foods. We had ordered all the jars and boxes of baby foods. Derek got all the right foods at the recommended times. By our second child, I did away with all those commercial supplies other than easy-mix dry baby cereals. As Jay started needing solid food, I had a hand grinder, and he ate mostly what we did. That worked well and was so much easier and more nutritious than all those store-bought baby foods. We did the same for the last two boys. Since we had dairy goats and laying hens during those years, and had plenty of excellent, wild-harvested food, our children thrived.

Over all the years with four rambunctious children, we never had a single broken bone, although there certainly were ample opportunities. I have always felt that their diet of fresh milk and eggs, plus plenty of fresh meat and fish were a strong contributing factor.

Medical Emergencies

Often I am asked how Jim and I managed to raise children hundreds of miles from any professional health care, and often with no one else around for added support. I maintain that it was simply by God's providence and common sense.

Medical emergencies did occur, yes, but both Jim and I had first aid training and were educated, sensible adults. Moreover, we had faith that God would provide whatever we needed when we were faced with difficult or dangerous situations. Probably

Jay, Isaac, Derek, Aaron in parkas made by Mom with all fur inside under the material covers we call snow shirts in 1983.

the most serious application of that training and faith was when our eighteen-month-old son Derek was severely burned when a mug of fresh coffee, just poured boiling out of the pot, was tipped over on him.

We were in our one-room cabin at our summer fish camp on the Colville River, the Niglik. It was early morning, on a very foggy July day. Jim, Derek, and I were still lying in our bunk built into the back wall of the cabin. It only took two steps from there to put the coffee pot on the propane stove. I had just poured two cups of scalding hot coffee and turned to hop back in bed, when Derek, who had crawled out behind me, reached out and grabbed the handle of a mug. It tipped over and spilled down his wrist and chest. As he screamed, my first reaction was to yank his white t-shirt off over his head, knowing it was holding the scalding coffee against his skin. The burn was so instantaneous that a lot of chest skin was peeled off with the shirt, but at least the source of the continuing burning was removed.

Our next action was to get something cold against the burned area. I soaked a washcloth in cold water and laid it against his chest while holding his wrist down in a bowl of cold water. I needed ice. We had no refrigerator or freezer. Jim took a bag and ice pick out to the riverbank where a lens of permafrost was exposed and chopped some ice out for me. With that ice, I was able to keep the cloth and water cold. Derek was screaming and I was crying with him. He certainly didn't want the cold water and ice touching him and, of course, didn't understand the reason for it, but it was necessary to help stop the burning.

We continued to keep cold against the burned area for several hours, then put burn salve and clean gauze bandaging on it. We had no antibiotics, so my biggest concern was the possibility of infection. We talked about flying in our plane to the nearest medical services, one hundred and forty-five miles away, but heavy fog prevented any chance of that for the time being. There was nothing more we could do but try to comfort Derek as best we could.

By late afternoon, the fog had lifted enough for us to fly the twenty miles across the delta to our family homesite on Anachlik Island. Located there was a runway capable of accommodating a larger instrument-rated plane. We were able to get ahold of an air taxi in Barrow and arrange for a plane to fly out, pick Derek and me up, and take us back to the Barrow hospital. By late evening we were there receiving medical help. Derek was immediately put on antibiotics to fight infection and his burns treated more thoroughly. However, the doctors claimed Jim and I had managed care of Derek and his burns extremely well with the cold water/ice packs "first care" methods.

Derek and I spent over a week in Barrow, staying with friends and receiving medical care daily at the hospital. Although I was encouraged to leave Derek in the hospital, I refused, worried that the added trauma to my baby did not outweigh my ability to care for him myself. As scar tissue formed over the burns, some third degree, Derek was given whirlpool baths daily and the dead skin was peeled off with tweezers. It was very painful and both Derek and I cried a lot. Thank God, no infection developed and after the medical staff in Barrow loaded me up with extra medication and bandages, we were allowed to return home.

Derek still has scarring on his chest and wrist to this day; however, the scab removal procedure reduced the scarring greatly and speeded the healing process, despite the pain.

The only other medical emergency with the kids requiring outside help was with our two-year-old Isaac the summer of 1980. It was a beautiful day outside and of course the kids were outside playing. I couldn't stay outdoors with baby Isaac continuously since I was cooking for a big crew boarding with us, so I had rigged up a baby harness and tied Isaac with a line to a big stump we used as a bird feeder, to keep him from wandering off out of my sight from the window, since he usually headed straight for the barn across the way to see our rabbits. He had lots of toys with which to play, plus a nice sandbox. I checked out the window often to make sure he was okay. At one point he was crying, so I went out and brought him back inside. He was not happy about that, for he dearly loved to be outdoors, but I noticed a small red spot on his wrist. I figured he needed more lotion and was crying from a mosquito bite. After spreading more anti-mosquito-bite lotion on him and letting him go back out, I didn't think any more about it. He was just happy to be back out "SIDE, SIDE," as he called it.

The next morning, Isaac's whole arm and hand were extremely swollen, alarmingly so. The area where the bite had been on his wrist was redder and so swollen that I couldn't even see any puncture mark, but we figured the swelling had something to do with that bite from the day before. What to do? The nearest medical facility was at the BP Petroleum Complex in Prudhoe Bay, about seventy miles away. Jim loaded Isaac and me up in the *Golden Plover* and we flew over and landed on the oil company's strip. A security person drove us over to their medical clinic and soon Isaac was being examined by their medic. After several attempts to get some medications down a small child, they gave up and said they had nothing but adult dosages and we must take Isaac to the Barrow or Fairbanks hospital. In retrospect, I am amazed that these medical people, or even myself, had not come up with the perfect solution. Open the capsule with the adult-sized portion of inflammation-reducing powder, reapportion the amount for a child, put the reduced part back in the capsule and get Isaac to swallow it. See, they had done the part of reducing the amount of powder, but instead of putting it back into the capsule, they had tried getting Isaac to swallow it by mixing it into honey, ice-cream, and other sweet things ... but it was so potent that it would still gag him and out it would come. Back inside the capsule would have worked perfectly! Oh, Well.

Consequently, our only choice was to take Isaac elsewhere. Off to Barrow I went again with a medical emergency. Isaac was in no pain, but the grotesquely swollen limb just looked terrible. At the Barrow hospital, Isaac was quickly given a shot of antihistamine to reduce swelling, and it was amazing how fast it worked. Once the swelling was down, we could clearly see the two little puncture marks on his wrist. It had been a spider bite! Once I had some spare medication to have on hand at home from then on, we returned home the next day. We have since learned that several family members have allergic reactions to certain foods or bites, and we must keep medications on hand at all times.

Homeschooling

As school age rolled around, Jim and I had to decide how to manage the children's education. We wanted the family to stay together, plus remain together at our homesite. Since much of Jim's education had been by correspondence and my family also had used correspondence homeschooling when we lived in Barrow, it was natural for us to go that route. Alaska had a state-run correspondence program headquartered out of its capital, Juneau, so I started Derek's formal schooling through that venue. He was now six and old enough for kindergarten. It was fall of 1978 when several boxes of school materials arrived by mail. This state-sponsored centralized school program was quite elaborate, even for preschool. There were teacher instruction manuals for multiple subjects. As a homeschool teacher, I had a lot of material to wade through in order to teach in the prescribed manner laid out in these instruction manuals. Derek did well right off, since he was not a stranger to books or education, being raised in a home immersed in reading, learning, studying, and hosting many highly educated guests from around the world who boasted much scientific expertise. Not only did Derek master the work quickly, but his closest little brother absorbed much of the subjects along with him. This later made early schooling for Jay a bit problematic, as he was often totally bored over his schoolwork since he had already learned most of the material with Derek.

We later switched to a more local homeschooling program. The state had developed regional correspondence divisions, and the closest one to us on the North Slope was the Yukon-Koyukuk School District (YKSD), located in Nenana, southwest of Fairbanks. Our local North Slope Borough School District had no correspondence division ... apparently, we were the

Isaac and Aaron with a box of school supplies brought by our advisor Sarah Drew from the Yukon-Koyukuk School District.

only family on the North Slope not living in a village already provided with a school. We petitioned the YKSD to take us on, even though we were far north of their normal service range. They accepted us and even provided an advisor, who would make home visits. WOW! This was one of the reasons we wanted to switch programs. We would have direct input from the school with home-delivery of supplies. It would no longer be only via mail.

Secondly, we had much more control over the school materials provided. The YKSD used the Calvert Homeschool program which was tried and true, simple, and condensed into basics. From this base, we could add whatever else we wanted. Only one box contained the books and materials for each grade. There was only one teacher's instruction manual which showed what must be covered from each subject per day. Simple, easy. So different from the State's centralized program which was comprehensive, yes, but very elaborate and extensive, considering it often was going to a little cabin in the bush. Although I am a college graduate and could manage it, I felt that a much simpler program was a better fit for most homes needing correspondence schooling. Calvert was perfect in this respect.

From the basic Calvert's courses, I added extra spelling books and expanded on other materials pertinent to each student. Plus, our kids were able to pick various endeavors to fulfill a physical education requirement. They often chose running their trap lines or cross-country skiing. All four boys completed most of their K-12 grades using Calvert's.

The boys had regular testing and assignments to complete for their counselor/advisor, who tried to make monthly or bi-monthly home visits. The advisor would fly to the Prudhoe Bay Oil Field, landing at the Deadhorse Airport, and then transfer to a small air taxi to fly to our homesite on the Colville River, sixty miles to the west. Sometimes Jim would actually do the flying with our own air taxi, Golden Plover Air. They would usually spend the night with us in order to have time to go over everything we needed to cover. New materials arrived and tests and completed work was picked up. One time our advisor actually arrived by charter helicopter!

One added aspect to our children's homeschooling was that each boy had at least one school year away at a regular public school. This was usually during middle or high school grades so they had a chance to interact with their peers plus experience group sports. When this happened, close family or friends would host a boy for the school months, and this took them to places like Washington State, Idaho, and North Carolina. Derek even spent part of a schoolyear with friends in Germany and attended a local German School where he was immersed in the German language, plus had the chance to tour other places in Europe.

Boys riding bikes on frozen fall-time tundra in 1992. It was unusual not to have snow on ground yet.

Aaron at his University of Alaska-Fairbanks graduation with his brothers left to right, Jay, Aaron, Isaac, and Derek.

All four of our boys graduated high school with honors and earned scholarships to continue on to college. Derek graduated with an engineering degree from the University of Alaska Fairbanks (UAF) and later became a registered professional Alaska State Engineer. Jay also graduated from UAF with an electrical engineering degree and went on to get his master's degree there, too. Isaac graduated from the University of Alaska Anchorage (UAA) with a degree in Aviation Management. Aaron graduated from UAF with a degree in Computers and Information Technology. All four sons continue to be solid contributors to Alaska's workforce and have never lost their interest in pursuing new things. I attribute much of that to their whole family's heritage and thirst for knowledge, always reading and studying books, insatiable curiosity ... always striving to learn more.

The family has often laughed at a comment Isaac once made as a young boy: "I don't need to go to school anymore. I already know everything I need to know." Even at a very young age, our children had absorbed a great deal of local knowledge about Arctic life and conditions, along with numerous worldwide environmental issues. Our many guests were amazed at their skills, knowledge, and confidence on a very mature level. Thankfully, we were able to convince Isaac that he still had a lifetime of learning ahead of him.

Chores

Chores day in and day out! Everything that needs to be done has to be done by us. Little is delivered or provided from outside sources. Shelter, heat, water, and food are the major requirements of all people, and those of us living in wilderness or isolated areas have to do all the work ourselves. We built our own homes, provide much of our food through subsistence hunting, and have created many extra amenities for a comfortable life. However, supplying heat and water are the primary daily chores.

Firewood

We heat our home with wood. How is this possible in a treeless land you might ask? Well, the Colville River has a very large watershed. Throughout much of that area willow bushes grow profusely. Each year the high waters of spring break-up wash huge amounts of driftwood down-river, resupplying the many accumulation points along the lower delta. Finding firewood starts by learning where these piles of wood are located, accessing them in winter when travel becomes possible and then hauling the wood home with sleds pulled by hand in the earliest days and now by snowmachines.

Sometimes we gather and stack driftwood in accessible spots during summer months for retrieval later, but mostly we find and dig wood out of the winter's snow with shovels on a regular basis. Jim's knowledge of the land helps him know where to look when the land is under a white blanket of ice and snow. Someone unfamiliar with the lay of the land could pass right by great accumulations of wood hidden under the snow.

Some of our firewood has even come from logs salvaged from the outer coastline or barrier islands where currents wash flotsam from Canadian waters far to the east. We have sometimes burned wood that had beaver gnaw marks on it that originated from somewhere on the Mackenzie River.

In more recent years, as the oil fields came closer to our home and roads provided access, we began getting cast-off dunnage for firewood. Tons and tons of various types of unused

Teena doing firewood collecting chores with baby Derek on her back under her fur parka.

wood needs disposal during construction of oil field work and facilities. This has become our major source of firewood in recent years.

After gathering firewood comes the sawing, chopping, and carrying into the house. This chore has changed little over the years for families who heat with wood. Some wood is made ready and stacked near the door as an emergency supply, but most is handled on a daily basis. The sawing was mostly done by hand buck saws in earlier days, but in more recent times, when much of the wood is large timbers, a chainsaw has been

Jim hauls firewood from oil company cast-off dunnage.

Isaac sawing firewood with Clyde standing by to "help."

added to the tool chest. All our family takes part in these wood chores. Winter has always required the most work.

While the boys were still living at home, they were major contributors to keeping our firewood well supplied and ready for the stove. Once they were all grown and gone elsewhere, that chore mainly fell back on Jim's shoulders completely. One winter day in 2008, I experienced a terrifying few minutes as Jim was outside preparing his snowmachine and sled to go pick up a load of firewood. I called this escapade "Dad's Wild Snowmachine Ride" as I later related the story to our boys in a message.

Dad's Wild Snowmachine Ride

I debated with myself about even telling any of you boys, but since Dad already threw out the hint that something happened yesterday, I'd better explain. He had a serious accident. I watched the entire episode helplessly from the kitchen window. From start to finish, it probably happened within only five-six seconds.

He started his parked snowmachine which was sitting in front of the Powerhouse door while standing next to it. It was still covered. The choke was open, and it roared to life but suddenly leaped into action with a lunge and jerk to the right as it roared off at full throttle.

In that split second, as it leaped past Dad, his right arm was snagged in the back cargo rack in a twisted, odd fashion and the sudden pressure exerted on his arm, locked his arm down and started dragging Dad behind the runaway machine. It careened across the planks of the walkway, through the willows, smashing a one-half-inch piece of rebar flat, missed a piece of stump on the lake's edge by a hair, raced across the thin lake ice, hit the far shore of the lake, raced on toward a three-foot-long piece of ten by ten dunnage lying in the grass, and hit it dead-center.

The engine finally died a split second after hitting the block of wood, but Dad was flapping like a rag in the breeze at the back of the machine the entire wild ride. As the machine hit the block of wood, it tipped just enough to finally allow Dad to wrench his arm free, so he was thrown down just as the machine died (stalled due to open choke) and the block of wood was thrown about ten feet to the left away from Dad. He fell down on his back and lay still a second but raised one arm to show he was still alive, knowing I had been standing in the window and was probably watching. He slowly got to his feet— thank goodness, no broken legs— and walked over to the snowmachine and got the cover off, started it, and drove back to the house by driving around the lake's edge.

Once in the house, I helped get his stuff off which was wet from snow driven into his boots and waistline. He was doing his "laughing in pain" thing, and he was already in so much pain from his arm and shoulder that he went into shock and got very cold. It was about an hour before the pain medicine he had quickly swallowed took effect and I had him covered with blankets in bed. The outcome was no broken bones, but badly wrenched and bruised shoulder and right arm. The back of his right hand, wrist and forearm are swollen where most of the pressure from the rack bar was exerted. His chest muscles, knees, and neck are very sore from the ground beating. I think his chest must have been banged against the back hitch. One blessing was that there was no sled attached. That would have made things MUCH worse.

I was shaking so badly, having watched from the window, I could hardly hold my spoon, as I had been eating some bean soup. I kept thinking (and still do) what would I have done if he didn't get up? No second snowmachine was handy—it would take a long time to get another machine out from summer storage—how would I get him back to the house, and then what?

You probably guessed that the throttle was stuck wide-open with ice in it. That new snowmachine is very powerful. I can just hear Aaron now, "See, that is just the kind of thing I've been afraid of!"

Dad is up and about this morning but moving slowly and gently. I thank the Lord that so many factors saved Dad from death or serious injury. It is a miracle that he has no broken bones!

This story was written to our sons in 2005 soon after the incident.

Winter Water Chores

Water is another basic requirement and needs to be obtained and transported to the house on a regular basis. During the winter months, this chore has remained about the same, although replenishing household water supplies in summertime became easier the day we bought a gas-powered water pump and hoses.

One of the most important advantages to our homesite on Anachlik Island is a deep, freshwater lake, the only one deep enough not to freeze down to the bottom by spring anywhere in the northeastern delta region. Our lake is over twenty feet deep in places and we believe it to be spring fed. By spring, the ice in the shallow lakes has frozen to the bottom so fresh water can no longer be obtained by cutting a hole through the lake ice.

After freeze-up, and once the lake ice is thick enough to support a person's weight while carrying buckets of water, a hole is chopped through the ice about ten feet off-shore, nearest the house. We use an ice chisel, similar to ice chippers, but this chisel has a smaller, very sharp cutting tip. Ice is chipped away in a circle about eighteen inches in diameter, large enough for a five-gallon bucket to fit down in the hole. In the early days before plastic buckets, the water buckets were clean five-gallon metal gas cans.

After reaching water, the floating ice chips are cleaned out with a shovel and fresh water is now shimmering in the hole ready to be dipped out and carried up to the house. Getting the water to the house is sometimes done entirely by hand, one or two five-gallon buckets at a time: dipping water from the hole, walking the one hundred yards, climbing the porch steps into the outer porch, through the inside door, down the hall into the water-tank room, and heaving the water into the five-foot-tall, thirty-inch-diameter water-tank, over and over again.

There are two connected indoor tanks with a total capacity of three hundred and sixty gallons. This water feeds a very modern water system within the house to the kitchen and bathrooms. A battery-operated pump, similar to systems found in RV trailers, runs the system. In the early 1970s, our first water tank was an open-topped fifty-five-gallon drum. Later, we acquired a larger tank and eventually upgraded to a set of two one-hundred-and-eighty-gallon tanks made from galvanized culverts coated inside with plastic.

To ease the labor-intensive water chores in winter, we developed a system of hauling water in thirty-gallon heavy-duty garbage containers, tied on a sled pulled by a snowmachine which could be driven up next to the water hole. The bigger barrels are filled at the water hole by dipping water with a smaller five-gallon bucket. Then lids are snapped on to keep the water from spilling out as the snowmachine pulls the sled up to the house. The water is dipped out of the barrels and

Hauling buckets of water from lake by snowmachine, sled, and large barrels to indoor tanks made from galvanized culverts.

carried by hand into the house. This speeded up the whole operation and eliminated a lot of extra steps between the water hole and house. Usually, two or three trips with the snowmachine and sled sees the tanks full.

Summer Water Chores

When temperatures rise above freezing in the summer, we devised a simpler way to get fresh water into the house. A small gas-powered water pump was set up by the lake's edge with a twelve-foot intake hose reaching out into crystal clear water. Several sections of discharge hoses are connected

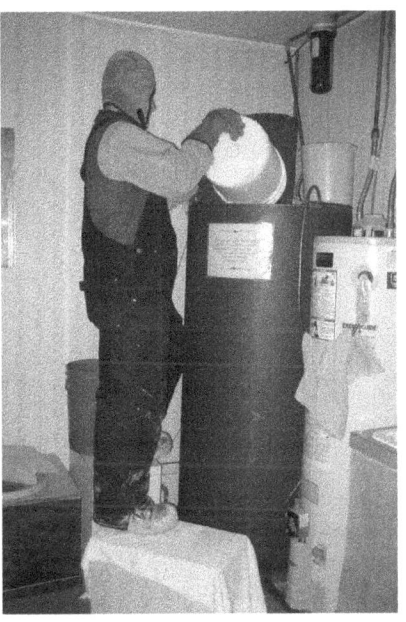

Jim pours fresh water into big indoor tank which is part of our modern water system.

together to reach all the way from the pump into the tanks inside the house. When water is needed, the pump is started and water gushes into the tanks like magic. At least two people are still needed for this method, since one person operates the pump, while another must hold the hose at the water tank end and give the signal to stop the pump when the tank is full. There have been a few times over the years when a miscommunication at the time of full tanks caused panic and a well-washed-down tank room.

More Chores

Two other chores for wilderness families are unavoidable: garbage and sewage disposal. Our household garbage has always been carried to a burn site away from the house where most all garbage is burned and what doesn't get completely consumed by fire is hauled off to the burial site.

We use "honey buckets" for sewage. Our toilets are built as a wooden box with a lid that lifts up to remove a five-gallon bucket. The lid has a regular toilet seat built right in. The bucket contents are dumped in a landfill, just as non-burnable garbage, and are buried. The permanently frozen ground (permafrost) does not allow for any underground pipes, nor do we try to keep above ground pipes (like under the house) thawed during cold winters—it would be a much too expensive proposition. Emptying the honey bucket is another frequent chore.

Our gray water (from sinks, bathing, and laundry) drains from the house through regular drainpipes into ditches that eventually carry the run-off to the river. These work even in winter, as long as we are careful not to allow liquid to drip out of the drains, but release it to go out all-at-once so the drains don't accumulate slow moving amounts of water.

Summer thaws release the buildup of winter's frozen gray water that accumulates below drains. I remember as a child in Barrow sliding on my little sled down the frozen waterfall of gray water from our house's bathroom drainpipe. This is not possible with our current home drains as they exit under our raised deck.

Another chore, done every winter after enough snow accumulates around the house, is to bank snow up around the lower sides of the house. This adds a layer of insulation against wind and cold and helps tremendously to keep the heat inside the house. Shoveling and packing snow against the bottom sides of the house seals off the air under the house, making it an insulating barrier to cold, and stops a lot of cold from seeping in through the lower walls and floors, especially during windy days. People living in cold regions have long known these tricks for added warmth: building snow houses or blocking snow around sod or wooden structures.

Raising four strong, capable sons was a blessing in a land that requires labor-intensive chores to maintain our lifestyle. We came to fully appreciate the reason farmers usually had large families. Plus, our family has never needed a membership in an athletic club to stay in shape, nor have we needed a set of weights to build muscles. Just daily chores kept us all fit.

Rabbit House Incident

Chores always included care of our many animals. In the mid-1970s, I experienced a serious problem while caring for our many rabbits in their little building. The story later became a funny experience about which we could laugh, but NOT at the time it happened.

I went outside to feed and water our rabbits in their Rabbit House, as we called it. It had a porch door and the second door into the inner room. I had left the outside porch door open, but, of course, closed the inside door. This proved to be a mistake, considering the wind was blowing gustily. Just as I was finishing up the chores and about to head home, I heard a crash on the porch. I went to open the inner door to see what made the loud crash and couldn't budge the door. It was firmly jammed shut. I then realized that the high wind blowing in through the outside door had blown a plank which had been leaning up against an inside porch wall against the door like a firm wedge. I banged, kicked and rattled the door over and over trying to dislodge the board. No luck.

I waited and waited, thinking someone at the house would miss me and come and check on why I hadn't returned yet. After several hours, I decided no one was coming to rescue me and started trying to figure out some way to get out. There was a window. Should I break it? I figured that would be a last resort. Meanwhile, I realized there was a small twelve by eight inch vent in the bottom of the door with wooden slats. I began breaking out the slats with a small piece of wood I had found. I figured that if I could get my arm out through the hole, I might be able to push the board out of the way. This eventually worked, but it took a lot of pounding and prying since the board was jammed quite tightly.

When I finally made it back to the house, no one seemed concerned. Jim was busy on some project, unaware I had been out of the house. Derek was just a little tike absorbed in play. Jay was just a baby. Well, maybe if meal-time had come and gone, I might have been missed!

Embarrassing Incident

This is not really related to chores, but worth the "chuckle. I was busy in the kitchen one day when my husband handed me a gift he picked up—a tube of pale green lip balm. Since my lips are often chapped and my nose was sore from a recent cold, I quickly smeared it around on my lips and tender nose and continued working. Soon afterwards we had unexpected company which I invited to stay for dinner. Hours later, when the guests were gone, I went to the bathroom and was horrified at the face that looked back at me from the mirror. My mouth and nose were smeared with bright red lipstick, and it must have entertained the guests with quite amusing speculations. What I thought was only lip balm was really a new lipstick that turns red after applying. Why none of my family discreetly informed me of my mistake has fueled a family debate for years.

Chapter 4
Family Hunting

Our Meat Supply

Hunting has always been a big part of our lives here in the Arctic. We need the furs for our outer clothing such as parkas, boots, mittens, and ruffs, but the meat is the most important. During our guiding days, game taken by our clients was usually our main source of meat; however, as we dropped out of the guiding business due to Jim's flying business, the family took over the hunting chores. And that is what it is—a chore that needs doing throughout each year as meat is needed. Every family member has participated, learning to stalk, shoot, skin, butcher, and care for the meat. Hunting is a chore we all enjoy because it involves fun outdoor activities we all love. Caribou meat has always been our staple meat. Caribou can be hunted any time of year, except May during calving season. They are plentiful. Dall sheep and moose are often hunted in the fall and supplement our caribou meat. Another favorite meat is muskox. We were only able to hunt those animals for a limited time between 1996 to 2004 when the North Slope had a permit only Tier II Subsistence Hunt. During those years, our family took one animal every year. It is superb meat, like the finest beef. I will relate a few of our past hunting adventures.

Teena's First Caribou

Although Jim had been hunting caribou since a young boy, my first caribou was shot at our summer fish camp on the

Teena provided dinner with her first caribou a few yards from our Niglik cabin.

west side of the Colville River Delta in 1970, my first married year. It was a hot day in July when the caribou herds roamed around the area almost daily and Jim and I decided we needed fresh meat. Jim and I simply walked a short distance from our little cabin, we picked out a big bull from the passing herd that had no other animals behind it, and I had a clear shot. I settled down in a prone position with an old favorite rifle propped up on a small mound of tundra in front of me and made my shot an instant kill. The other caribou were not even alarmed, but only ran off a short distance as we got up and walked over to the downed animal. We confirmed its demise and then walked back to the cabin to have a cup of tea. It was our standard practice to wait about twenty minutes before starting to skin and butcher our game. This allows the meat to tenderize on-the-hoof.

Fresh caribou meat just harvested by Derek and Aaron.

We carried a few plastic bags back out and I watched and learned as Jim quickly and expertly butchered the bull. We bagged the meat and returned home. Most of the meat went into our deep-freeze cellar, but the heart, tongue, and liver were held back for immediate use—delicacies we were eager to eat.

Over the years, I learned to skin and butcher game, but never came close to matching speed and skill as my husband and sons. It seems my skill mostly got lots of practice back at home with cutting and packaging meal-sized portions of meat after hunts. I've always maintained that more work is involved in that job than the actual hunt.

Muskox Hunt

During the subsistence hunting seasons, our family applied and received one muskox harvest tag a year. We all applied, but only one tag per family was allowed, so we took turns during the years that muskoxen could be taken here on the North Slope. Isaac was the first family member to draw a tag for a Tier II Subsistence hunt for a muskox, which was located east of Prudhoe Bay on the Saviovik River. I accompanied him on that late March hunt where we had a winter-style camp and drove our snowmachines. Isaac shot a big bull and we had a fun adventure. Later hunting seasons opened closer to our home on the Colville River.

Aaron helps Mom cut up meat for dinner from a frozen piece of caribou leg.

What follows is the hunt for my second muskox, taken in the summer of 2001 on the Itkillik River, a tributary to the Colville River, about twenty-five miles south of Anachlik Island via river travel. As soon as the hunt season opened, Isaac and I packed all our camping/hunting gear in our small seventeen-foot skiff. We had to keep our gear at minimal levels due to having the small boat. Our bigger boat, the Carolina Skiff would have been nice to have but it couldn't have easily gotten up the shallow river to which we were headed.

Isaac and I left at noon on Wednesday and reached the mouth of the Itkillik River, a few miles above the turn-off to Nuiqsut, about 2 p.m. The Itkillik is a tributary to the Colville River, joining it several miles above the delta. As we motored upriver, we stopped often to climb up on the riverbank and scout around. We had a pretty good idea there were no muskox in the delta (except a small herd west of our island, which we couldn't hunt), but we didn't want to miss something.

We stopped at the mouth of the Itkillik in order to walk up on the bluffs west of the river to glass around. I waited at the boat for Isaac to return and report on what he saw. Once back, Isaac said we'd have muskox meat for dinner and that he could see lots of caribou.

We headed upriver on the Itkillik then, and it wasn't long before we were spending more time creeping along at an idle with the motor on tilt, or Isaac actually pulling the boat along through the shallows at every crossover of the river. Past experiences had taught us that at each major turn of the river, the deeper water shallows out and spreads out over the gravel. One wonders where all the water had gone from the deep channels, a lot must travel through the gravel.

Periodically we would stop, climb the bank, and look around for game. We worked our way upriver for nearly five hours, never seeing the herd of muskox again that Isaac had located from the mounds near the mouth. Sometimes I would get out of the boat to lighten Isaac's work and walk along the sand bar until we got to another deep-water spot where the motor could be used again. We were pelted with light rain several times. At 8 p.m. we stopped at a nice flat spot and set up camp. We built a fire, heated our tea water and ate our cup-of-noodles. No fresh meat. The riverbank was about twenty feet high along part of the river near our camp spot, and three high mounds within easy walking distance. Isaac walked to one nearby mound to get a better look around. He was sure we were just getting further away from the muskox, which must be hidden in a low spot. There were four caribou on the back side of the mound. It was time to settle in for the night though. We would continue in the morning.

The night was pleasant, no more rain, and in the forties Fahrenheit. We had two tents, because Isaac had his new sleeping-bag-sized tent to try out. My two-man tent held me and our gear. We slept well and, in the morning while I drank coffee and wrote in my journal, Isaac walked to the further mound to scout around. He spotted the muskox not too far away on a ridge and could see where they had been hidden the day before. We had only to go back down-river one turn to be in hiking distance to them.

We packed up camp and headed out by 10:30 a.m. We pulled the boat up at the proper spot and Isaac carried the 30-06 and a few other things while I carried my little pack. I was using Martha's famous one-shot-kill rifle that Jim's mother had given him. It took us about two hours to make our way downwind into position. We had to cross through tall willows at the

Our first Tier II Subsistence Muskox bull harvested in March 1996 by Isaac

river's edge, and then walk through muskeg, around the far side of a large lake, to the northwest edge of the ridge which circled around the far side of the lake. We could see some of the muskoxen standing about a half mile further down the ridge to the south. When Isaac glassed the herd from the top of the ridge, where we began our walk just below the ridge, he could see the majority of the herd moving around just back of the ridge-top, out of my sight. We could clearly see the big bull and a few other animals on the skyline. I think the bull was watching us moving along but didn't seem alarmed.

We worked our way toward the herd along the base of the ridge between ridge and lake. It was slow going for me. Isaac had to stop and wait for me often. The muskoxen dropped out of sight, and a bit further on, Isaac climbed the ridge to see what was happening. The bull and other animals had all lain down just over the top of the ridge. Ironically, we looked back toward the big willow patch near where the boat was pulled up out of sight below the bank, and low and behold, there was a big muskox bull walking along. We discussed going back for that one but decided to stay with the ones we were already close to. The other bull seemed to be walking purposely northwest, and there was too much of a chance that he would outwalk us and be long gone by the time we could retrace our path. But we still marveled that we must have walked right by that bull when we first got out of the boat.

Once in line with where the herd lay, we crawled up the fifteen-foot bank. I was following Isaac and had discarded my pack about fifty feet back, after Isaac said they were right ahead. Once up on top, we could see the entire herd lying down only about seventy yards away. Isaac got me all set up with the gun propped on his coat and a small grass hump, and then he raised up enough to study the different animals to locate the big bull we'd seen. From my prone position, I could not see any heads well enough to identify sexes or sizes, only big furry bumps.

Isaac found the bull that had a blond mane, and he had several dark females lying next to him. I got ready to shoot the animal Isaac said was the big bull. Now, we needed to get them to stand up. My arms were about to give out holding the rifle ready. Isaac got up on his knees. Then I got up and could see most of the herd and heads clearly. I got in the prone position again, and then Isaac had to stand and loudly whistle several times before they began to stand up. The cows that stood up watched us but didn't seem alarmed at all. Finally, the bull stood and gave me a clear shot. I didn't hesitate. I didn't think my arms could hold the rifle steady much longer, even though most of its weight was supported by the coat and hump of ground. I aimed just below the tallest part of the hump, back of the front shoulder. I don't think he ever completely stood up, but lay right down again almost in the same position he had been in. Several cows moved in around him, so we couldn't even see if he was solidly hit at first.

After about ten seconds, we stood up and began walking toward the herd, now all standing. I suddenly remembered my camera was back down the bank in my pack. Isaac ran back for it. By the time he got back, the herd had moved away from the prone bull and formed their traditional ring, with the adults facing out in a circle and all the calves and young animals inside the circle. Then they began walking away, somewhat maintaining the circle. I tried getting some pictures of the herd, but none turned out well. One actually shows the herd to one side and the bull lying in the tussocks on the other side, but they were too far away to be a good picture. The herd did not gallop away until we walked right up to the bull and were standing there about fifty feet away. I turned my back to speak to Isaac and look closely at the bull, turned back and the herd was totally out of sight. They had to run only a short distance to be down over another bank into an old dry lakebed, which they followed around at a run

Teena adds to the family meat supply.

and were gone. Later I walked over to the edge of the bank to look for them and they had gone clear around the far side of the ridge out of sight.

Except for some blood coming from the nose due to a lung-shot, the bull looked like he was still sleeping as we first saw him. It had been a quick, clean kill. We took some pictures. Isaac called his dad back at Colville Village with his little cell phone via a tall relay tower within line-of-sight in Nuiqsut, about fifteen miles away and told him I had taken my muskox and asked about weather and the possibility of flying into the big lake below us and exchanging Derek for me. I was exhausted, plus would be little help carrying meat back to the boat. (It is illegal to use the plane to hunt or transport subsistence-taken game.) Derek was home for a few days between jobs and would help Isaac carry meat to the boat while Jim flew home with me. Weather was OK, so that was the plan. (It is amazing to think about being able to call home with a small phone from way out in the middle of "nowhere" on the Arctic prairie.)

Isaac is an expert at skinning and butchering animals and the job was done in about two hours. Fortunately, the pack back to the boat for the guys was much shorter around the downwind end of the big lake, compared to the route of our upwind stalk.

It was a day and a half before Derek and Isaac made it back home in the boat. They had camped another night and added a few caribou to our meat supply and maxed out the boat. Since it had rained a lot while they were gone, I was glad to be back home, although I love to go boating and camping and hated to miss the last part of the trip.

Chapter 5
Challenging Life on the Colville River

C-46 Cargo Plane Saga

A story of interest in these early years of our Colville Homesite development occurred in winter of 1974. It was when our family chartered large cargo planes to bring the year's supplies into the homesite and also backhaul our commercial fish to market in Barrow and Fairbanks. That year, Jim's parents, Bud and Martha, were living in Fairbanks during the winter months so their younger sons, Mark and Jeff, could attend public school. The folks did all the arranging of the supplies and cargo flights from their end in Fairbanks and Jim was in charge on the receiving end of the flights here on the Colville. One flight turned out to involve the most amazing set of circumstances we ever experienced in all the years of flying in supplies.

To begin with, we had a number of extra people living here with us that fall and helping with our commercial fishing operations and all the various activities of daily life. My brother Mark Wartes and his wife Denise and baby son Marwan lived here on the Colville with us at the time, plus my close friend Brenda Smith and a young man, Roy Nieman, were here. We ran many nets and caught thousands of pounds of whitefish during the fishing season, so much of this product needed to be transported to market. These fresh-frozen fish were sacked or boxed up as whole, individually frozen fish. They were stacked and made ready for transport to market when our annual supply plane came from Fairbanks. We also

C-46 cargo plane on Colville River in 1950s bringing supplies to Helmericks. Visitors came by dog team to see the incredible sight.

had to ready empty fuel drums and propane bottles to return to Fairbanks. Some years there were other backhaul items, like trophy hides and horns taken by our hunting clients from earlier in the fall.

Another job in preparation for a cargo flight was building a runway out on the river ice, since our dirt runway was too small for a large plane like a C-46. Jim had to choose the best location on the river right out front of our property and spend many hours clearing snow off the ice to create a smooth surface about five thousand feet long for the big-wheeled ship. This was done with the small tractor in the beginning, and then in later years, with the John Deere 350 tractor. Once the runway was done, then drums were lined up along each side from one end to the other about one hundred yards apart, thus giving the pilots a clear view of the runway's position and length. We used flare pots on top of the drums for light in dark hours. These had to be lit by hand and were shaped like large, hollow cannon balls about six inches in diameter with a wick sticking out of the top. We filled them with diesel fuel. We also used forty-two-ounce cans with rolled up pieces of burlap as wicks. Someone would have to drive up and down either side of the runway to light or extinguish these flares before and after a plane landed and took off. Once the runway was made, it had to be maintained until the flights were over, which could be several weeks long, so if the wind blew, the runway needed re-plowing to remove any snowdrifts.

We had no radios to communicate with airplanes; neither did we have phones or radios to communicate with people on the Fairbanks end of the supply-run. Jim drove the approximately fourteen miles to Oliktok, the closest place that had a phone available at the military DEW Line site called POW-2. This trip took at least an hour each way over rough ice or frozen tundra with a snowmachine. From there, Jim could call his parents in Fairbanks to get and give the latest news. We also could get messages from Jim's folks over a regular broadcast radio station that aired personal messages twice a day, morning and evening. However, this was not foolproof, due to occasional bad radio reception. But it was the best we had in those days.

Teena's Journal

11-12-74 We got a message from Dad tonight saying the C-46 flight is planned for the 19th. The message came over message hour on KIAK radio station from Fairbanks.

11-18-74 We were up early and doing all the pre-flight preparations for the C-46 flight due in tomorrow. Fish bags and boxes, drums, propane bottles, and trophies were all loaded on the two tractor sleds [thirty-foot and twenty-foot] and then pulled down to the river by tractor and positioned beside the ice runway. It was after 8 p.m. when Jim and Mark were finally done, having worked straight through all day with only a short break to eat. [Mark and Jim were the only guys here now, since Roy had returned to Fairbanks earlier.] I did daily chores of feeding the dogs, checking fox traps across the river, and the usual house and baby duties. Plus, I sawed enough firewood to last for two days, since tomorrow is expected to be extremely busy.

11-19-74 We got up at 6 a.m. and Jim went out and put heat on the tractor. The radio message last night said the C-46 would arrive at 10 a.m. We all got ready, [which meant tractor running, dressed in outdoor gear, snowmachines ready to drive out on the river, and outgoing mail ready] but soon fog and low overcast skies made the flight questionable in our estimation. However, we waited in a state of readiness until 11 a.m. before concluding the plane wasn't coming. At some point over the next few days we got another radio message saying the next C-46 attempt would be on the 23rd.

11-23-74 Jim got up at 4 a.m. and put heat on the tractor ... the plane was due in at 9 a.m. We all went out to the runway to meet it, but after waiting about one-half hour, we all came back to the warm house.

11-25-74 Jim got up at 4 a.m. again and put heat on the tractor, but by 6:45, we heard a radio message that the flight had cancelled. Later in the day, Mark and Jim drove to the DEW Line site to call Dad to order snowmachine parts for Mark's snowmachine, in the hope they could come up on the next flight. Plus, both guys asked Dad to order new snowmachines for them from the Shontz Store in Barrow to be picked up and returned to us on the C-46 backhaul, after delivering fish to Barrow. [The normal routine was that the C-46 brought supplies from Fairbanks to us here on the Colville, we reloaded the plane with fish that was then flown to Barrow, drums of fuel that had been delivered by supply ship earlier in the year and other supplies from Barrow were then loaded on the plane and flown back to us on the Colville. Next, the plane was loaded again with fish and the rest of the backhaul to go back to Fairbanks.]

11-26-74 Again Jim got up at 4 a.m. to put heat on the tractor, but at 5 a.m. he woke me to tell me he was very ill with dizziness and nausea. We think he had gotten carbon monoxide poisoning from driving the snowmachine yesterday with the broken muffler. I got up to help watch the tractor. Jim started it at 7 a.m. in-between lying down to rest. The plane was due in at 11:30 a.m. and Jim felt well enough to drive the tractor down to the ice runway by then. Mark, Denise, and I drove down to the runway by snowmachine shortly before the arrival time. [Both Denise and I carried our babies on our backs under our parkas: Marwan at seven months old, and Derek almost two years old.] We all waited beside the runway for about half hour before returning to the warmth of the house. By 12:30 p.m., we had given up hope again for the day and went about our usual daily activities. [That night our radio message on KIAK told us the flight was rescheduled for Saturday, the 30th.]

11-30-74 Up again at 4 a.m. to begin another C-46 Day. Again, we went through the usual routine and again waited to no avail.

12-03-74 Another scheduled C-46 flight today, and we proceeded as usual with Jim up at 4 a.m. and subsequent preparations for a 10:30 arrival. But again, NO PLANE! Today was the 6th failed attempt. The evening radio message from Dad told us that the plane had actually started to leave Fairbanks today, but lost oil pressure in one engine and aborted take-off.

12-04-74 We had another C-46 morning of preparations. Again, no plane. After lunch, Jim got ready to go check his trapline. I was outside feeding the sled-dogs when Brenda ran up to me and said a big airplane was circling us. [Not sure why I hadn't heard it. Maybe it was the barking dogs.] It was the C-46, and it came in and landed. It was about 1 p.m. Jim had just put the tractor away, so he ran and got it started again and quickly drove down to the ice runway. Mark and I dashed for a snowmachine and drove to the runway also. Dad and Jeff [Jim's youngest brother] were aboard besides the pilots. Dad gave us the story of woes from his end of the stupidity and incompetence of the air service's operation. After taking four hours yesterday to get the plane loaded (and this was with heavy equipment to help), the oil lines on the plane froze up, thus the loss of oil pressure when the plane was ready to take off. Then this morning they were ready to take off when the pilot discovered the gas tanks were low. The company personnel had drained gas from the plane's wing tanks to fill the space heaters that were keeping the plane warm while sitting there on the ground. So, a fuel truck had to be called to come refill the wing tanks, taking several hours. The circumstances for all the previous cancellations and delays were all just as ridiculous. We were able to unload the entire load in forty minutes, all by hand. [The only mechanized equipment used was the tractor and one snowmachine to pull sleds up below the big cargo door. Supplies were handed down to us to stack on the sleds. The outboard plane engine was kept idling for heat on the -30°F day.]

[All our non-freeze groceries were frozen, so Dad asked us to make a list of it all so it could be replaced, or we could be reimbursed by the air service for the loss aboard the plane during the delays. It was cases of fresh eggs, fresh produce, can milk, pop, and other things.]

By 3 p.m., the plane was reloaded with several hundred bags of fish for Barrow, and it took off, with Dad aboard. Jeff stayed with us on the Colville, and helped Mark and Jim load the big tractor sled with another load of fish that is for Fairbanks. At 6 p.m. the flares were lit in preparation for the returning C-46 from Barrow. We waited and waited! Jeff kept the flares filled with fuel, but we finally gave up and picked up the flares at 10 p.m. We fell into bed exhausted at about 11:30 p.m., wondering what had happened to the C-46 this time.

12-4-74 The morning's radio message said that, "the C-46 lost an air cooler and is down at Lonely; everyone is okay." [This was another DEW Line site called POW-1 between Colville and Barrow, and the message gave us no indication whether this happened enroute to or from Barrow. It turned out to be on the return from Barrow.] At 11 a.m., Jim left for the DEW Line at Oliktok to call Dad at the Lonely DEW Line site to find out what was happening. When he got back, he told us that another C-46 bringing parts for "our" C-46 was due to land at Lonely at 4 p.m. and if all went well, they hoped to be back to the Colville by 9 p.m. [At this point, to add to the problems of the delayed flight, Jim had problems with equipment. He couldn't get the tractor started due to battery problems, so had to start our small portable generator in order to use the battery charger. To his exasperation, that generator wouldn't start, and he had to take it apart to trouble-shoot the problem. He discovered a rusty magnet, sanded it clean and reassembled the generator. Now running, Jim was able to put the charger on the tractor battery plus also rig up a bright electric flood light on top of the house for added visibility of our place for the approaching plane.] Jim finally had the tractor out on the river waiting for the flight to come in and all the flares were lit again shortly before the flight was due. We waited and waited! Jim drove the tractor back about 12:30 but kept it running. Jeff picked up the flare pots about 1 a.m. Jim and I finally lay down on top our bed with our clothes on in case the plane suddenly showed up.

12-6-74 No message heard this morning. Jim had kept the tractor idling all night, but soon put it away. In the evening, a message from Mom in Fairbanks said that the C-46 was returning direct to Fairbanks, and we were to listen for a further message concerning how Jeff and Brenda were to get to Fairbanks. [Jeff was missing school and Brenda was scheduled to return to her home in Washington State.]

12-7-74 We heard no message about any flight, so went about our day. The guys went trapping and gathering firewood until mid-afternoon. Around 5 p.m., we heard a C-46 fly over us and circle the buildings. The guys rushed out and lit the flares. [In December, the sun is no longer rising above the horizon at all.] However, the plane did not land, but flew on to the POW-2 DEW Line and landed on the big runway there. [We could see this by watching the plane lights.] Jim debated as to if this meant we were to take Jeff and Brenda over there, but we decided to wait a bit to see what might develop. About an hour and a half later at 6:45, the C-46 took off from the DEW Line and returned to the Colville complex, circled twice, buzzed low over the runway and came around again and landed. With the guys all out at the runway, Denise, Brenda and I sat at the house wondering what in the world was happening. I was getting ready to walk out to the runway when Jeff drove up on a snowmachine to get Brenda for leaving on the plane. We all went along to hear the story of what had been happening. Two days ago, the crippled C-46 from Lonely had unloaded our thirty drums of fuel from Barrow while at Lonely but had kept our two new snowmachines and mail aboard and attempted to fly to Deadhorse. However, more mechanical problems forced them to land at the Oliktok DEW Line, POW-2, where the snowmachines and mail were off-loaded. Remember, this is the DEW Line about fifteen miles from our place.

The plane then made it back to Fairbanks in the wee hours of this morning. Dad got another plane in the afternoon to fly north again. This plane is the same one that circled and then went on to POW-2 at Oliktok. It landed there to pick up the snowmachines and mail and bring them back to us. The guys had off-loaded the snowmachines using large planks for a ramp out of the cargo door. Now the plane needed loading with all the fish for Fairbanks stacked on the big tractor sled up by the house. It would take too long to try and heat the tractor, so we all worked hard to move all the fish bags by snowmachine and small sled. A platform was created halfway up to the cargo door of the plane by laying a sheet of plywood across the top of four fuel drums. Fish bags were handed up from snowmachine sled to a person on the plywood platform and that person threw the bag on up to someone standing inside the plane. These are seventy-to-ninety-pound bags, mind you. All of us girls helped right alongside the guys. The plane was loaded, Brenda and Jeff aboard, and on its way back to Fairbanks by 8 p.m. What a big job!

This story was gleaned from Teena's daily journal of November 1974

The biggest irony of the whole ordeal was over the tractor. Jim had worked so hard heating and having the tractor ready for days on end that when the plane finally did show up unexpectedly to be loaded, we didn't have the tractor ready. The tractor pulled the loaded sleds of fish right up to the cargo door and the sacks could be loaded directly from the sled, which acted like a loading platform in itself. The heavy sacks had to be handled twice as much without the tractor.

To conclude this saga, there were later attempts to retrieve the thirty drums of our fuel left at Lonely, but the several attempts I mention in my journal failed due to bad weather. I

Tractor with big sled used for loading fish sacks to fly to market. Jim unloaded hay for our goats to haul up to barn with snowmachine and sled.

never found further reference to them, and do not remember if we ever got that fuel. Another note is that we experienced many flight delays during the years we chartered large cargo planes to deliver our supplies, but never to this degree.

Building our New Home, Lodge and Museum

Jim and I finished our first home on the homesite in early 1970s, added a sunroom, and lived there until 1988. With all our business requirements and four growing children, we then built and moved to a new structure on the far southwest corner of our lake. This large structure not only became our new home but had a whole section dedicated to housing our many guests plus another part for the continually expanding museum. It was over five thousand square feet and two-and-a-half stories.

Looking northeast, Colville Village with lake on left and east channel of Colville River on the right. The center building is the new museum/lodge/ house. The runway is in the upper left. Buildings in the foregound: the rabbit house, barn, hanger, guest house, and other outbuildings. Buildings in the distance are the original buildings.

It became known as the Helmericks Lodge and Museum. What started as a small single-family homesite had escalated into what is now called Colville Village, a three-generation family homesite.

The story of how we built the Home/Lodge/Museum building includes many curious and sometimes amazing events. It took several years to obtain enough materials to begin construction, and many of these materials were gleaned from cast-offs from the nearby Kuparuk's oil field construction projects. In the winter and spring of 1986-87, there was an ice-road to our property. This was because the oil companies needed water from our freshwater lake as ice-roads were constructed for their westward expansion during the winter exploration season. This ice-road gave us the opportunity to haul in many needed supplies. One day I happened to be in Kuparuk and noticed several big eighteen-wheelers loaded to the hilt with wood getting ready to head south off the Slope. I asked one driver where he was going.

"We've been contracted to backhaul all this scrap wood to the Livengood dump since it's less expensive for the oil companies to dispose of it this way."

I looked at all that wood and realized there was potential for salvaging a lot of usable building materials, besides what

Looking at the lakeside of our home/lodge. Walkway extends from the southwest end of the runway to the house.

could simply be used as firewood for our stove. I told the trucker, "If you follow me about eighteen miles west of here, you could get rid of that whole load and then travel on down the Haul Road with an empty trailer."

This was quite a revelation to the truckers, since they had already been paid to dispose of the wood, and once I explained where I wanted them to take their load—to private property nearby—they jumped at the chance to hasten a speedier southbound trip. The ice-road across the normally unpassable land and river to our homesite was the key!

I called ahead to Jim at home to get our front-end loader, a John Deere 644, ready to unload thousands of pounds of wood. This scenario was repeated a number of times once the word got out that we would take the wood. There was quite a bit of scrap for firewood, but mixed in were usable plywood, finished two by four and two by six lumber, and big timbers.

It took the family several years to sort the pile of scrap wood. Our boys did most of the work. We had to carefully disassemble many four by eight shipping crates made with full and half sheets of plywood. The bottom of the crates was made with four by four lumber and thick planks that eventually were used to make walkways between buildings on the homesite.

Our buildings are between the river (above) and lake (below).

Our house/lodge/museum with riverside porch in 2012 after new paint job by Derek.

This salvaged lumber became an integral part of our new house/lodge. Many exterior base walls and the base roof had product words stamped across the plywood.

Another feature of this new house that came in part from salvaged oil field lumber was the creative wainscoting I made for our second story great room, a part of the museum. We had received many large, empty wire-rolls that had beautiful new wood centers of beveled one by six slats. Once taken apart, I was able to stain, varnish, and construct beautiful, sculptured wainscoting. A special re-purposing of scrap wood.

Another unexpected feat during the building of our new two-story house occurred during the initial framing in the late summer of 1987. The building labor was done mainly by just our family members. It was slow and exhausting for Jim, me, my parents, and our four boys working many hours every day.

We had reached the point of raising forty-foot-long trusses. Jim had been building every truss single-handedly as my father cut each piece of wood with templates he had made. We had no lifting equipment to start raising the trusses onto the second story walls that towered twenty feet in the air. We discussed having to build time-delaying scaffolding and considered what else we could do to save construction time.

Teena's plants and muskox rug in northwest corner of upstairs Greatroom. Door opens to a eight by sixteen foot sunroom full of more plants and big windows.

Our home in July from the SW side of our lake with Jacob's Ladder flowers.

That same evening, four canoes pulled up along our homesite riverbank. It was an extended family—nine adults—just finishing a river adventure. While discussing with Jim about flying them to Deadhorse, they noticed the new construction. Two of the adventurous party were accomplished contractors and they asked if they could help while they waited for weather to clear for flying. Jim explained our dilemma over raising the trusses. The two experienced men said, "No problem. With all the workforce on hand presently, and our expertise, we'll get them up!"

And we did. It was an amazing feat of putting the first four trusses in place, which created a firm foundation to which all the other trusses could be added later, one by one. This included the expert craftsmen balancing on twenty-foot-tall walls. It was truly an unexpected blessing.

A point of interest to many guests is how nice all our homes are including all the amenities available to most modern homes, such as the usual appliances and a water system. Besides well-insulated, two-story homes, we have built hangers for our planes, garages, shops, a barn, and other "out" buildings. Small generators have supplied all our electrical needs. We have had to bring in diesel fuel, aviation and motor gas, and propane for our various fuel requirements. All of these things make for as comfortable and pleasant a life as possible.

Some people have felt that because we live in such a remote wilderness, it is ridiculous to go to such lengths to have all these conveniences. We feel just the opposite. We love our independent but grueling lives, with freedom to be as industrious as our abilities allow. Why not work hard to build modern homes and provide whatever conveniences possible? Coville Village was our home-base even though it was always fun flitting around here and there between homes and camps depending on what activities were on the agenda.

Communications on the Colville Homesite

When I first came to the Colville, our means of communications were pretty limited. There were no phones

Looking west, our lake is in the middle of the Anachlik Island with the original buildings midway along the northwest side of runway. The east channel of the Colville River is to the left of the island.

and radio contact was only by two-way aircraft radio with limited range. We could receive messages sent by regular AM broadcast radio.

The only ground-based aircraft radio was a big two-way radio in Jim's folk's house that they used in the 1960s for passing weather and other information to airline pilots who traveled between Barrow, Umiat, and the DEW Line Sites along Alaska's northern coast.

Alaska had several broadcast stations like KJNP in North Pole and KIAK in Fairbanks that had special programs for sending messages to people living far out in the wilderness. Trapline Chatter on KJNP was the service we used when family or friends needed to get a message to us from Fairbanks. Of course, it was only a one-way communication, but better than nothing. The person sending a message could only hope it was received.

Trapline Chatter aired over KJNP twice a day, early morning and late evening. Our reception on the North Slope wasn't foolproof due to atmospheric interference at times, but messages sent to us over this AM radio station were often a critical link in communications, such as when Jim had to fly one of the planes to Fairbanks for maintenance. His messages to us on Trapline Chatter were the only way for us to know he was safely there or get news as to when he was returning.

The news of the birth of several of our boys was announced over this radio program. I remember the message to Jim the spring of 1976: To my dad, Jim Helmericks on the Colville River ... "I arrived at 4:11 p.m. this afternoon, weighing 6 lbs. 11.5 oz. Can't wait to see you. Love, your new son, Jay Gregory Helmericks."

Trapline Chatter was a lifeline to people living remotely who cherished news from their loved ones, whether good news or bad: news having cheerful greetings like happy birthday wishes, birth announcements, engagements, weddings, or sad news like deaths, divorces, or illnesses. All of life's joys and sorrows were aired across radio-land on a daily basis.

If we needed to contact people in Fairbanks, we had to drive by snowmachine to our closest neighbors at POW-2 site, or the DEW Line site at Oliktok, fourteen miles northeast of our homesite. There was a phone we could use, often to order parts for broken-down equipment or for planning our annual cargo flight. This was a minimum of two to three hours round-trip.

We often went for weeks, occasionally months, with no news from family or friends, only general news and music on AM radio stations whenever reception was good, mainly during dark hours.

Communication systems and technologies in Alaska keep improving. Eventually, by the late 1970s, we were able to get a radio-phone service that sent a signal to Fairbanks by radio waves and then connected us to the land-line phone system. This service was a great improvement over the one-way communications of Trapline Chatter. However, it was costly and NOT private. Since all conversations were broadcast over a single-sideband radio on a frequency anyone with a radio in range could monitor, everyone listening heard everyone else's conversations. This was somewhat like the situation with Trapline Chatter, but now two-fold with conversations both ways. Everyone knew everyone else's business and news, good or bad.

As the Kuparuk Oil Field grew and expanded west, closer to us, more opportunities for improved communications opened up. We spent thousands of dollars over these years experimenting with various radio and phone systems as they came along. We purchased radio-phones, like one called a Bag-Phone, which transmitted signals to communication towers in Deadhorse or Kuparuk facilities. These were more private, but also more costly. Besides the cost of the equipment, we paid a minimum of $1.00 a minute for calls.

In the late 1990s, we bought a radio-phone system that we were able to use to operate a regular phone. The transmitting radio part of the system broadcasted to our companion receiving radio on a tower in Kuparuk. There the signal was patched directly into a phone network. Later we bought a digital wireless phone system that would also give us email and internet services. Some systems worked and some didn't.

These systems eventually gave way to more advanced phone systems and eventually the cell phones, as communication towers spread across the Slope. Now, there are few places here on the North Slope that do not get cell reception. Most systems were contingent on oil field facilities within signal ranges and the cooperation of the oil company involved. People were always helpful. Thanks to a tower and nearby structures installed for oil field operations, our current phone and internet connections provided by GCI Communication Corp. are very technologically advanced.

It is amazing how our communications advanced in less than fifty years. Cell phones work across much of the North Slope now and other satellite phones and internet connections are in all villages, petroleum facilities, and even remote camps. I can now sit in my kitchen at our homesite and talk face to face with my mother down in Washington State or a son working in Antarctica! Or I can go on a muskox hunt forty miles upriver from our home and call home on my cell phone to report that all is well. We have continuous cell phone and internet connections to family and friends, plus social and news networks. There have been times in the past when we even had satellite TV, although now our Internet connection replaces any need for TV. We can access live programming and videos any time, twenty-four hours a day via our Wi-Fi system.

In addition to radio/phone-type communications, we often had single-sideband radios set up to communicate with field camps across the North Slope. The birth of our third son, Isaac, was relayed to Jim through one of these radios via a camp that also had a satellite phone. We were often used as a relay station between research camps and phone services elsewhere, in Barrow to the west or Prudhoe Bay to the east.

We also had CB radios for communications between our house and anyone traveling in our truck away from home. For a period of time, this was our main safety backup for traveling over remote and dangerous ice trails. We had strict check-in times and contingency plans in case someone needed help.

In the early days, our mail was delivered to Barrow, the closest Post Office. From there, we were responsible for picking it up ourselves or arranging delivery by an air taxi. Usually this was coordinated with transportation of our commercial fish to markets in Barrow. We would deliver a load of fresh fish with one of our own airplanes and then bring mail back home. Or we would charter a Barrow plane to bring our mail out to our homesite and it would backhaul a load of fish to Barrow stores. The sale of our fish would at least cover the expense of getting our mail home. This arrangement of backhauling fish to market also worked well for covering the expense of chartering a large cargo plane to bring supplies from Fairbanks.

Our mail usually came in twenty-pound to forty-pound mailbags filled with personal and business letters, many catalogs, cassette-tape letters, small packages, and the usual junk mail. When we subscribed to various newspapers, there would be piles of those corresponding with how long it had been since the last mail. We did a lot of shopping from mail-order catalogs, so big and little packages in the mail were common.

Jim and Teena by C-206 on floats. Teena is wearing her fancy parka made from the Arctic ground squirrels she trapped at Sheep Camp.

For his first four years, our son Derek only knew his Wartes grandparents through photos and cassette-tape recorded letters that arrived in the mail bags. He also had one other unusual connection—knitted and crocheted socks my mom made and mailed to him. When he was finally able to meet them for the first time, it took my mom knitting a pair of socks while he watched for Derek to finally realize who she was. "Oh, you are my 'Knitting Grandma!'" he exclaimed in delight.

Pilot's Wife

Patience is a virtue, especially when faced with lack of communication and delays.

I am the daughter of a man who flew off into the wild spaces of the Arctic and wasn't heard from for days on end, and the daughter of a mother who trusted God to take care of her husband when he encountered dangerous situations. With that background, my life as the wife of a pilot was somewhat of an easy transition. However, no matter how brave I tried to be, life still held many stress-filled days of waiting and wondering where my husband-pilot was—safely down on a lake or sandbar waiting out bad weather, or some scarier alternative? I would have to bolster my resolve to trust God, as my mother had done, and believe Deuteronomy 33:27 that states: *The eternal God is your refuge, and HIS everlasting arms are under you!* This was also my dad's motto during all his flying days.

I remembered one time when my father was overdue for several days during the days my family and I lived in Barrow in the 1950s, a headline in the Seattle Times said, "Most Lost Man Lost again!" My dad's hometown newspaper was announcing that Bill Wartes was missing on a flight across Arctic Alaska, again! Of course, later news explained that he had not really been lost, but simply out of radio contact while waiting for the fog to clear so he could fly home. My mother was used to playing the waiting game, and she became a great inspiration to me.

An unforgettable dream I once had was indicative of this inner, God-given peace I would call upon when my husband spent so many hours in the air, and especially when he didn't return home on schedule. In my dream, Jim was getting ready to land the *Golden Plover* and as he circled around the landing pattern, the engine suddenly quit, and the plane began to career to the ground. I gasped in fright, but an amazing thing happened. That plane's wings began to flap like a bird and caught the fall and the plane glided safely down to stop on the runway. This dream became my solace.

Jim did have a few close calls with mechanical failures, but always managed to make it down safely to the ground and then get repairs. Usually, he was able to relay news back to me at home on the Colville explaining the delays.

Bad weather was the cause of most delays, and if Jim was in a town, he could call or radio me. However, there were many times when he was forced to land and wait out bad weather where there was no way to communicate his location and situation to me, as in my father's day. Sometimes he was only a few hours delayed from the planned flight time, but other times he was gone for several days.

One of these situations occurred when returning from a bird survey along the Alaskan coast. On the long return flight, they were suddenly surrounded by dense fog and had to quickly land on a nearby lake. Being on floats in summer is a great advantage when flying across many areas of the North Slope since water is everywhere. Jim and his survey client spent several days camped in a survival tent that was carried in the plane while they waited for the fog to lift. I had to wait also, since Jim had no way to communicate with me. His plane radio could reach no radio stations in order to relay a message to me that he was down safely and awaiting better weather. I could only trust he was okay and safe.

One time this same scenario happened, but Jim was able to contact a passing jet and the pilot was able to relay a roundabout radio message to me that all was well.

Transportation

Transportation in the early days of the Helmericks Homesite was limited mostly to air transport, as I've indicated earlier. Other than a few overland treks from Barrow or Prudhoe Bay with tractor-trains (cat-trains), everything arrived in airplanes, such as with the many cargo-plane flights that delivered all the materials for the first house in 1956, and my tale of the extreme circumstances of the C-46 cargo flight in 1974. There were no roads near the Colville River, although gravel roads were springing up around the Prudhoe Bay Oil Field sixty miles to the east, and the Dalton Highway (nicknamed Haul Road) was built in 1975.

In the early 1980s, the Kuparuk Oil Field was expanding to the west toward us from Prudhoe Bay, making the extensive oil field road system useful to us. This gravel road system was connected to the Dalton Highway, which follows the pipeline to Fairbanks and then on south to Valdez. At the opposite end of this road system is the road to Oliktok Point, the northwestern point of land bordering the eastern side of the Colville River Delta. This road was completed to access the far northwestern Kuparuk well pads and build a dock and water treatment plant to supply processed water for the oil field. Oliktok is a point of land on the Arctic Ocean coastline and approximately fourteen miles from our homesite on Anachlik Island in the northeastern section of the Colville River Delta. This became a jumping-off place for us to access our home by driving out over the ocean ice and then into the mouth of the river delta in the winter. This made having road transportation practical for the first time, better winter travel during the months our planes were hangered during the cold, dark winter.

In 1984, we bought a 2-wheel/4-wheel drive pickup and had it driven up the Haul Road from Fairbanks. It was driven from Prudhoe Bay, west across the new Kuparuk River bridge, through the Kuparuk Oil Field, out the Oliktok Road to Oliktok Point, off the road and over the four-foot bank onto the frozen ocean ice, southwest along the mainland shoreline into the eastern channel of the Colville River Delta, wound through a maze of small sandbar islands, and up to Anachlik Island and our home. At this point, we had to create and maintain a ramp up onto the island, since there was a four-foot to five-foot rise.

With this new truck and road access, we now had another way to transport supplies home and move commercial fish to market. Deadhorse, the service area at the northern end of the Haul Road and the location of the public airport, became our hub of transportation. Road access to the Post Office and other supplies delivered by commercial trucks or jets was a positive step for our remote lifestyle. We were no longer limited by only air transport into our home runway. We also had this same road access even in summer by leaving our truck parked at Oliktok at winter's end, just before spring break-up of the ice. We could still get to the truck with our small planes or by boat, if travel by truck was necessary.

Because Jim was the family pilot, I became the designated driver. We bought a truck canopy to protect gear and supplies in the truck bed, plus give us shelter while traveling if needed. We bought a double-axle trailer for hauling even more supplies with the truck. I usually made several trips a year along the Haul Road between home and Fairbanks. Southbound, I usually had sacks of frozen fish going to markets along the way, such as in Wiseman, a small community along the Haul Road about halfway to Fairbanks. Northbound, some of my loads included lumber and other building supplies, propane bottles, a canoe, a satellite dish, bales of hay and animal feed, and occasionally livestock like goats, chickens, and rabbits.

In the fall, usually around early November, the river and ocean ice would become thick enough to support the weight of a small truck. Jim would check ice thicknesses by driving his snowmachine along the route we would drive from home to Oliktok. He would follow the coastline closely where the ice would freeze down to the bottom first and safest. Jim would chop a hole through the ice until he hit water or ground to verify how thick the ice had become. Of course, this thickness was contingent on prior weather, which varied every year, although the time frame remained within a fairly consistent window. Once we had a minimum of twelve inches along the whole route, we could start driving the truck over the ice again.

Early in the fall, this was fairly straight forward, with not many obstacles like deep snow to negotiate. However, as the winter wore on, snowfall and high winds that drove the snow into deep windrows of hard drifts began to make these drives more harrowing. We never traveled without a shovel, for getting stuck was commonplace. Even with a four-wheel drive vehicle, a snowdrift across the trail could stop you, even if you picked up speed to try and force your way through it. Sometimes you'd make it, as snow flew off in all directions. It all depended on snow thickness and width across the drift. More often than not, you would grind to a halt. You had to get out and start digging snow, making a tire-width path in front of each tire to make a way through. You did this over and over, moving a short distance each attempt, until you finally broke free. If the drift was so deep that you became high-centered from the underside of the vehicle, it meant a lot more digging. I have spent many hours digging my way out of snowdrifts over the years of driving over the snow-covered ice. You obviously had to have daylight to negotiate the trail after the latest windstorm, so you could drive around the worst drifts, but sometimes avoiding one drift put you straight into another one you couldn't avoid. It usually took several hours to drive the fifteen-mile route.

One time I was forced to dig my way out of a deep snow drift with a hub cap, thanks to an unknown person who borrowed my shovel from out of the back of my truck and forgot to put it back. I got stuck and found no shovel where it was supposed to be! I was left puzzling out what to do, until the idea of removing a hubcap and using it as a shovel came to mind. One learns to be innovative when there is no other recourse. It was slow and backbreaking, but it worked. You can be sure, I never traveled again without making sure I had that shovel!

One obstacle for transportation to and from our island in winter by truck was the three- to five-foot banks off the mainland at Oliktok and those at our island riverbank. Negotiating up and down these banks to get on and off the ice meant creating a firm ramp. At Oliktok, we sometimes had help getting a pull or push from an equipment operator from the DEW Line site, or they helped us by building a good ramp. Otherwise, we had to shovel snow in front of the tires, drive up a foot or so, let the weight of the truck pack the snow hard, backup and shovel more snow, drive up again a little further, shovel more snow ... continuing this until we had a firm enough ramp to get all the way up the bank. Here at home, we would lay down planks or water-down a snow ramp. These ramps constantly needed maintenance, mainly due to winds creating snowdrifts across them. More shoveling chores!

Deep cracks in the ice were a danger for which we had to watch when driving over the ocean ice. Stress cracks would form in certain areas along the route we took to Oliktok and could open up suddenly due to water pressure under the ice. They were usually not too wide to be able to drive carefully across—such as two to eight inches wide—but if they opened much wider than that, we carried planks that could be laid down over the crack on which to drive over. These cracks opened and closed indiscriminately, and we had to keep a close watch for them in certain areas.

The last major obstacle to traveling out over the river and ocean ice is overflow, which effects both truck and snowmachine travel. The overflow we face is when water comes up on top of the coastal ocean or delta river ice, usually due to high winds creating tidal surges. As these winds create increased pressure under the ice, they can force water up through cracks to the surface. Depending on location and ice conditions, this water can be several inches to several feet deep. Sometimes the weight of the water bends the ice down, creating pockets of water on top of the firm ice. Normally, this water will recede as the wind decreases, or just freezes as a cap on top of the existing ice. Not such a big deal unless you are trying to drive over an area with fresh overflow with a truck or snowmachine. Then it can be very dangerous.

If visibility is good and you are familiar with the characteristics of that area, you might be able to just drive around the overflow. However, it may not be seen at all in the dark or can become obscured by snow or thin ice. Even though there is solid ice below, you risk getting stuck in slush and then become wet trying to get unstuck. The danger comes in getting wet while in freezing weather and not being able to get dry and warm again quickly. What if you are far from a heat source and your truck or snowmachine quits, leaving you stranded?

Both Jim and I have had episodes of unexpected overflow complications on a trip across the ocean ice. One time, I was driving home along an established truck trail from Oliktok late one night in the dark. Visibility was extremely limited due to blowing snow, but since I had a good trail to follow, I thought I could make it with no problem. We were having high southwest winds, so I knew I needed to watch out for overflow. About fifteen minutes out on the trail, an isolated dark spot loomed up in front of me in the headlights, so I swerved to the left to avoid it, thinking it was overflow on the ice. I'm not sure what actually created that dark area, perhaps a small section of ice that was snow-free, but what I turned directly into was a deep pocket of overflow under the snow. Plop! I gunned it, trying to get back up to solid ice, but to no avail.

Fortunately, I had Derek with me who was a strong teenager by then. Together we worked over an hour with a shovel and chunks of wood for traction to make our way out of the slush-filled depression. Water and slush were up to the bottom of the truck doors. We were cold and wet by the time we got the truck back to solid ice. About then, I looked up to see a light coming. Jim to the rescue! We always had strict protocol for departure and expected arrival times when traveling in dangerous conditions. Jim knew we were late and must have encountered problems. He had come down the trail looking for us. I was proud that we had gotten ourselves out, but thankful to know Jim had come to help if we had needed it.

One comical outcome to that event became clear when we had to drive back out over that same trail the next day in daylight and good visibility. We had quite a laugh as we drove by this one spot in the trail were someone had obviously veered suddenly off the nice flat trail and fell directly into a pocket of overflow. Whoever it was obviously thrashed around quite a while to get unstuck and then made their way back up onto the trail again. What could have possibly made a person do that?

Another such episode was one Christmas Eve in the late 1980s when Jim was trying to get home during a break on a job in the oil field. He had a load of mail, Christmas presents, and dunnage for firewood. It was dark out, a bad time to be negotiating across the expanse of ice to get home, but he was eager to be home for Christmas. A southwesterly wind had been blowing which can create overflow, so Jim was wary. Blowing snow and terrible visibility made seeing the trail ahead very hard. He had not gone very far out onto the ice from our off-road ramp at Oliktok when he encountered a large pocket of overflow. He was badly stuck before he knew it, by himself, with no way out except whatever he could devise on his own. The slush was well over a foot deep. He had to get the truck back up onto firm, dry ice.

That night, Jim worked over four hours in the cold and slush to get unstuck. You can't shovel slush. All Jim could do was put chunks of wood under the tires and drive up on them over and over in order to slowly make his way through the slush back to firm ice. He often had to use the jack to lift the truck, wheel by wheel, up onto the pieces of planks. By the time he got the truck back out of the overflow, he was cold, wet, and exhausted. He was still a long way from home, so he decided to go back to his starting point in Prudhoe Bay, spend the night, and try again in daylight the next day. However, the next day proved worse, with even more overflow blocking the way home. In the end, Jim left the truck on the road system to bring home another day and chartered a helicopter to get home. Having Jim home for Christmas turned out to be a very expensive, but cherished present for us all.

Our first truck served us for over twenty years. It did not travel a record-breaking number of miles, but the majority of its miles were hard ones over rough gravel roads or across rougher brackish ice trails. The truck had to be repainted one year to deal with rust problems. It had to have wiring replaced due to an engine fire. We replaced tires nearly every year as a safety precaution. We added extra lights for better visibility in adverse weather. It carried us back and forth to the Greater Prudhoe Bay area for mail and supplies many times a year, plus up and down the Haul Road many times. We sometimes had to relay big loads of supplies with our tracked vehicle, when conditions were too dangerous to drive the last few miles into our homesite with the pickup truck towing my two-axle trailer.

Although our old truck was still running, we bought a second truck in 2007 to continue our truck travels. Since many circumstances had changed by then, we rarely drove this new truck out over the ocean ice. We wanted to protect it from saltwater damage and the ravages of ice-trail travel as much as possible. The Kuparuk Oil Field had expanded to the point of having an oilwell-drilling pad which was connected to the road system within five miles of our homesite in the delta by then. We started parking the truck at this pad and then we commuted to and from home and the parked truck via snowmachines. This added a new element to our travels, but worked well as long as the weather allowed outdoor travel. There were limiting weather conditions for any kind of travels away from home, such as high winds with blowing snow, overflow, fog, whiteout conditions, or extreme low temperatures. Minus 30°F was our normal cutoff for outdoor travel.

A good example of how the road system changed much of our transportation methods, especially in winter, can be shown by telling of a typical mail/supply trip to and from Deadhorse. Prior to having a truck and access to the road system, all mail and supplies were obtained via air transport, our own or

Above: My Haul Road load is transferred to our ATV Tracktruck due to dangerous conditions on the river for my truck in 1989.
Middle: Refueling along the Haul Road with newly-painted old truck.
Below: Tracktruck and load headed across the last few miles to our homesite in 1989.

chartered. More recently, a typical winter trip to the post office to pick up and deliver mail is a day-long expedition.

There is a period of several weeks to a month in fall-time when we are unable to cross the frozen river ice because it is unsafe. Once it freezes thick enough to support the weight of a snowmachine and sled, we can drive over to the mainland and make our way to the closest oil drilling site that is connected to the permanent gravel road system. This is where we leave the truck until we need to travel to Deadhorse where the post office is located and we obtain other supplies. There is no grocery store there, but we can order groceries and other supplies from Fairbanks to be delivered there to pick up. We park and cover the snowmachine and transfer to the truck for the rest of the seventy-mile drive to Deadhorse.

Once all the errands are done, getting home is a reverse of getting out. We never make the trip without returning with a worthwhile load, which may include scrap firewood for our stoves, propane, or other needed fuel, along with the mail and other supplies. The drive and transfer of goods between truck and sled coming and going is always time-consuming, and sometimes the weather deteriorates and especially the snowmachine part of the trip can turn harrowing, as some of my snowmachining tales relate.

One such snowmachine incident for me was on my departure from home. One winter when I had to cross the river to get to my truck on the road system, I experienced a new lesson on what can happen with overflow. Even the river channels at the face of the Colville River Delta can be impacted by ocean tidal surges and we knew there was overflow out there, but it had not yet increased beyond a few inches deep and covered only a small area. However, it did cross my normal snowmachine trail. Jim assured me it would be safe to drive through, but as I encountered it, I made the mistake of speeding up to get through it quickly. I did not know how much pressure the water could exert on my skis. I was not holding onto the handlebars securely enough and my skis were jerked sideways and the snowmachine tipped over into the water. I was thrown into the shallow water. My mittens, boots, socks, and bottom edge

*Our new
truck was
usually
parked at
a nearby
drillsite five
miles east
of house.*

of my parka got wet, and I picked myself up and stood there looking exasperated.

Fortunately, this happened only several hundred yards from the edge of our island and our house. Jim was watching me leave and he jumped on his snowmachine and was soon out to help me get my machine back upright and then sent me back to the house to put dry things on. It was too dangerous to continue the five miles I had to drive wearing any wet clothes. It was well below 0°F Of course, it delayed my start for the day, but it was a lesson well learned.

With the advent of ice-roads came another means of travel that could get us even closer to our home island. As the oil field has expanded toward the west across the North Slope, reaching the Colville River Delta and beyond into the National Petroleum Reserve (NPRA), many ice-roads have been constructed which have provided access to the all-year-round roads. These oil industries' winter ice-roads, constructed and used from January through May, have been a big help to us in recent years for winter travel and for hauling supplies directly to the house either with our truck and trailer or delivered by contracted suppliers. Some of these ice-roads have spurs directly to our lake for its freshwater supply, thus giving us direct access to a smooth road, or they come near enough to still be useful to us for our own transportation needs.

The petroleum industry uses the ice-roads to explore for future oil and gas potential in areas inaccessible by the year-round road system, off the beaten path, so to speak. Built over land or water, they create smooth roads that will melt away in summer and leave little evidence of the passage of many vehicles. Water or packed snow are laid down over a designated path, mapped out earlier by surveyors, in layers which are allowed to freeze in order to build up many inches of ice for extra strength over underlying thin ice and for the protection of fragile tundra. This extra thick ice can support the transport of heavy equipment that needs to be moved to exploration sites.

Living at the face of the Colville River Delta put us near the route of many of these ice-roads, so they often gave us a means to more easily haul our own supplies or come and go

Ice-roads have become common and closer to our homesite.

without the strenuous snowmachine relay part of travel to the road system. With an ice-road right to our property, we could get our yearly fuel supply hauled directly to our large holding tanks and get other supplies delivered at much lower costs. One year, we even had my year's grocery order delivered right to our back door. It consisted of hundreds of pounds of canned goods, flour, sugar, and other bulk food, which came north on the Haul Road from Fairbanks on a weekly truck delivery service that supplied food for the many oil field facilities across the Slope. That was a momentous day, considering the contrast of labor and great expense of getting such supplies by chartered planes from Fairbanks in years past.

Machinery Woes

The more mechanical equipment and motorized machinery we had at our homesite to help with daily life and various operations and projects, the more headaches there were. A snowmachine pulling a sled is capable of transporting a great deal more than a person simply pulling a hand-sled. However, operation of mechanical equipment becomes more complicated by extreme cold, no heated garage, no quick access to parts. We had to do everything by ourselves as we learned to operate, maintain, and repair equipment: generators, heaters, snowmachines, tractors, front-end loader, air compressor. Living out in the bush means learning to be self-sufficient and innovative—learning to be a mechanic, plumber, electrician, sheet-metal worker, and welder—an overall problem-solver.

Complications arose with so many jobs. We often had to conduct ten other tasks just to get back to what we started out to do in the first place. In reviewing my journals, I am amazed at all the maintenance issues with which we were constantly plagued over the years here at the homesite. One of the main issues for us was the heating of our planes, tractors, snowmachines, and other equipment used in everyday work, since we had no heated garages or buildings to house equipment that needed warmth to start. Just getting the heating equipment to run, like a space heater, was sometimes a challenge. Tarps or blankets were often used to wrap around things. Snow blocks were built for windbreaks. Occasionally, we had to use a camp stove and pieces of cans or stovepipe to direct the heat where needed. It was always a time-consuming part of the workload of daily life during the cold season.

Before any roads, like the current oil field roads on the North Slope, most travel overland was carried out in the winter when the land and water was frozen. At that point, you can go anywhere, but it isn't easy traveling. The wind beats the snow into rock-hard drifts of snow. Consequently, working with equipment like tractors and snowmachines in this land where the ground can be frozen like jumbled concrete is very hard on machinery. Add the cold temperatures and you have conditions ripe for extreme wear and tear on equipment. Transportation overland like this was never a sure thing. Many a day, one of the the riders had a long walk home in sub-freezing weather because of an iced-up carburetor, or broken parts on the tractor or snowmachines like mufflers, motor mounts, belts, bogie wheels, skis, throttle cables, or another part. There never seemed to be enough spare parts, no matter how well one planned ahead. This meant many delays in getting the broken-down equipment fixed. Getting new parts usually meant a long wait, since most equipment parts had to come from Fairbanks or further south and be flown up with sporadic mail deliveries or in our own planes. It seemed that hardly a day went by without someone working on repairs to one or more pieces of equipment used for the winter clean-up work we were doing or just normal everyday activities.

For example, one day in late winter of the early 1980s, Jim needed to get our Piper Super Cub, the *Golden Plover*, out of the hanger. It should have been a simple job of several hours. The plane was parked inside the hanger behind several pieces of heavy equipment, our tractor and front-end loader. The hanger was not heated, so to get any equipment running required heating the engine. We had a diesel-fueled, forced air heater with a long hose to direct heat where it was needed. It was moved into place to put heat up under the tarp wrapped around the tractor engine. It wouldn't start! Troubleshooting the problem uncovered a broken wire.

Finally, with that repaired, the tractor was heated, started, and moved. Next the loader needed heat. While that engine was heating, another problem surfaced. One of the huge loader tires had gone flat and broken the seal at the wheel-tire bead. It turned out the air compressor was down due to a broken part, plus a new O-ring seal was needed for the loader. This meant a snowmachine drive to the nearest phone at the DEW Line Site, fourteen miles away, to order parts. Several days later, Jim had to make a trip to Deadhorse to pick up the shipped parts. The air compressor got fixed, but then the tire was too cold to cooperate in resealing, so more hours were spent covering and heating the tire to make it pliable enough to be manipulated by chain-binders and forced back in position to seal. Finally, the loader was moved out of the way and Jim was able to get the airplane out where he needed it to be, ten days later! These were the kinds of hassles that were common when working with equipment, especially in our cold environment. Life at our homesite required a great deal of patience and ingenuity.

As snowmachines began to rise into prominence in Alaska's outdoors, so did mechanical headaches. If you lived near repair shops, it wasn't so bad, but out in remote areas, you had to learn to repair these machines on your own. If you had to start them in extreme cold, the problems increased. If you drove them across the hard-packed snow on the Arctic prairie, you experienced many broken springs or other parts. These machines had many advantages to the old dog-team method of transportation, but when they broke down, they couldn't take you home like a dog-team could.

Jim spent many a winter day repairing an engine on my kitchen floor, where he could work in the warmth of the house. Reading shop manuals and learning to do repairs were necessary skills. Sometimes Jim had a long walk home, like the day he forgot his usual spare drive belt.

Contaminated fuel is one of the biggest problems in equipment operations that constantly needs careful attention. Fuel has to be carefully strained or filtered for water or contaminants each time a piece of equipment needs fuel.

Chapter 6
Our Livelihood

Scope of Our Work and Services

Jim worked for his dad in his younger years in many of the family enterprises, which included commercial fishing, guiding hunters and adventurers, guiding and consulting for many different companies, including those that were flooding to the Arctic for the growing North Slope petroleum industry, and flying for the air taxi service. Some of these enterprises date back as far as 1949, when the Helmericks commercial fishing first started. Jim's father, Bud, began a commercial fishing operation on the west side of the Colville River Delta at a place called the Niglik. Jim began running this operation by himself when he was a young teenager at thirteen.

Later, Jim started his own companies and worked mostly through these: the Golden Plover Guiding Company and Golden Plover Air. Through these companies, Jim and I continued to operate a big-game guiding business, both summer and winter commercial fishing operations, and an expanded air taxi. We went on to develop birding tours, Arctic adventure tours, Arctic consulting, and lodge accommodations.

As we moved more toward ecotourism, the hunting part of our guiding business slowly faded away until we no longer offered big-game hunts. Since the Colville River Delta is the hottest birding location on the North Slope, we began conducting birding, photography, and other environmentally-oriented

ARCTIC ALASKA ADVENTURES

Birding

Sightseeing

Abundant Wildlife

Remote

Wilderness

Photography

Flightseeing

Boating

COLVILLE VILLAGE

COLVILLE VILLAGE is the private homesite of the Helmericks Family, who are veterans of Arctic Alaska. The village is located about 60 miles west of Prudhoe Bay at the mouth of the Colville River Delta on the edge of the Arctic Ocean.

The NORTH SLOPE is a rarely seen or experienced part of Alaska. The ecosystem is truly unique, full of natural wonders and a truly fragile beauty hard to imagine without seeing it for yourself.

Pages from Arctic Alaska Adventures brochure.

Birding

Our home lies in the northeastern part of the Colville River Delta which is a superb birding area during the open-water season. In summer, with 24-hour daylight, the air rings continuously with bird songs. Since we are next to the ocean, we have both waterfowl and shorebirds nesting nearby. The area is made up of coastal tundra with lots of small ponds and sedge-grass marshes. Unique polygon ridge formations are prominent throughout. Large lakes also lie within the delta, making a very productive and varied habitat for nesting and migrating birds. Some of the more unique nesting birds that can be found near our home are:Yellowbilled and Pacific Loons, King and Spectacled Eiders, Sabine's Gulls, Arctic Terns, Bairds Sandpipers, and Snowy Owls.

Other local summer residents include:

Red-throated Loons	Parasitic Jaegers
Black Brant Colony	Pomarine Jaegers
White-fronted Geese	Golden Plovers
Oldsquaws	Black-bellied Plovers
Pintails	Dunlins
Glaucous Gulls	Ruddy Turnstones
Tundra Swans	SemipalmateSandpipers
Willow Ptarmigan	Rock Ptarmigan
Pectoral Sandpipers	Red-necked
Red Phalaropes	Phalaropes
Lapland Longspur	Snowbuntings
Hoary Redpols	Savannah Sparrows
	Short-eared Owls

Birding is done locally as well as on field trips. Knowledgeable bird guides are available to assist you whenever you desire.

Some spring migrants and occasional summer residents include: Buff-breasted Sandpipers, Stilt Sandpipers, Long-tailed Jaegers, Long-billed Dowitchers, Semipalmated Plovers, and Yellow Wagtails. A few of the rare birds at the Colville include:

SPRING	FALL
Ross'Gull	Ivory Gull
Bluethroat	Siberian Accentor
Northern Wheatear	Arctic Warbler
Barn Swallow	Orange-crowned
(Asian Form)	Warbler
Rufous-necked Stint	Sharp-tailed Sandpiper
Ruff	
Stellers Eider	
Emperor Goose	

Seasonal Specials

June

Nesting birds with breeding males singing and displaying—a tundra emerging from winter's sleep with amazing vegetation growth and early miniature flowers already blooming—24-hour daylight—little caribou calves running beside their mothers . . . .

July

Incredible numbers of baby birds everywhere - tundra plantlife in full growth with prolific flower displays - caribou herds numbering in the hundreds often ambling by just outside the lodge door - the Arctic's warmest days . . . .

GOLDEN PLOVER   GOLDEN PLOVER
AIR   GUIDING

Arctic tours. We operated these tours under the name Arctic Alaska Adventures.

Another reason we stopped guiding hunters is because Jim's flying began to take the majority of his time in the mid-1970s and Colville Village, a name our homesite had acquired, became "home-base" for the air taxi and the many other environment-based activities that served clients from all over the world.

This led to our homesite becoming the hub of research and environmental studies going on along the coast of the mid-Alaskan Arctic during the 1970s and 1980s. We were ideally located between the northernmost point of North America (with the town of Barrow) and the Canadian border. We had the means to provide services to all entities seeking to study various aspects of the Arctic Alaskan coastal areas, and we had vast knowledge of the area from many years of living here, including daily journals that had detailed information on all the flora and fauna.

Every time we turned around, we were contacted for information or asked if we could offer support to some new project involving wildlife research (birds, foxes, caribou, muskoxen, moose, fish, insects), archeology, tides, off-shore currents, air-monitoring, vegetation, climate, aerial photography, and many other studies.

Studying conditions in the Alaskan Arctic has become big business. Part of the reason for this was the burgeoning mineral, oil and gas development activities and government agencies wanting to study and keep track of what this would mean to the affected environment. Federal, state, and local governments were soon requiring many studies to be conducted as conditions for companies to receive development and operating permits. Baseline studies were needed and follow-up studies after activities began.

The Helmericks local knowledge, experience, and records became very valuable to the many environmental studies conducted across Arctic Alaska. Having spent many years as hunting guides, and subsistence users, a great deal of experience was cultivated with all the animals and game across the Arctic, including sea mammals out on the pack-ice of the Arctic Ocean. Sharing this local knowledge of the Arctic flora and fauna, plus our weather records and collections documenting Arctic life and conditions has always been an important part of our lives.

Our two planes together on the SW end of runway: Golden Plover on giant tundra tires and Cessna 206 Stationair.

Some results of this strong commitment to environmental awareness were the development of our extensive museum, plus our volunteer work of daily weather reports for the National Weather Service-Alaska Region for over thirty years.

Our homes, out-buildings, and sometimes even tents supplied housing for many of the research groups. I often cooked for large crews working out of our place. We supplied boats and other necessary equipment for work around the Colville River Delta. We often maintained our runway year-round for small aircraft. Providing supplies, ground and air support, and local expertise kept us very busy, especially in the warmer months of the year.

Jim and his father had flown small planes throughout the great expanses of the northern Alaska regions since the early 1950s and knew the land and ecosystems intimately. Their flying skills and knowledge became renowned within the scientific community and became sought after for the many studies that escalated over the years, especially as the Arctic came more and more into the limelight with the discovery of oil.

Jim became very busy with his air taxi, Golden Plover Air, flying aerial bird and wildlife surveys across the Arctic. Environmental companies loved using him for his flying skills, excellent safety record, and also because no one could match his observation skills for being able to spot game that even the surveyors aboard his plane would miss. Besides aerial surveys, Jim used both his planes to provide support to many remote field camps across the North Slope.

The Cessna 206 was the bulk or heavy hauler with skis, wheels and floats, and the *Golden Plover* on giant tires was almost like having a helicopter that could land anywhere, from tundra, gravel bars, offshore barrier islands, to dry lake beds.

After operating a commercial fishing business in the Colville

Golden Plover Air patch

River Delta since the late 1940s, our knowledge and records gave fish biologists invaluable baseline information to preface their later analysis and examination of the fish populations and habits along the Alaskan coastal and river systems.

Jim's love, knowledge and written records of birds in the Arctic regions have been extremely helpful to all those conducting bird studies. His

Jim could land most anywhere with his Golden Plover on 35" tires.

photography skills have added to this vast information base which Jim willing shares with others.

We supported so many people and organizations by providing lodging, meals, equipment, radio communications, and aerial flights that we started referring to each group by code names like "the bird people," "the fox people," "the bug people," "the caribou people," and so on. There would often be multiple projects and studies, which are listed in the appendix, going on simultaneously.

Three guest books are full of the names of visitors who have come to our house for just coffee and a short visit, a tour of our museum, or stayed longer as lodge guests. Just from 1975 to 1991, we had hundreds of visitors from thirteen different countries, and forty-three of the United States. Some visitors missed signing our guest book, as did frequent local visitors from the village of Nuiqsut, twenty-two miles up the Colville

Our C-206 flew hundreds of hours on floats during its busiest summer season.

See Jim's photos on his photography website: https:// goldenplover. zenfolio.com

River from us. Often repeat visitors have enjoyed looking back through our guest books to find their names from previous visits or just check for other guests they may know.

During the extremely busy summers of the 1970s–1990s, I often had a live-in helper. Feeding and caring for so many guests, as well as the family duties was exhausting! When possible, I had a teenaged girl come north for the summer to share in the burden of work. A niece or friend's daughter who was up for a thrilling adventure would arrive in spring and stay through late summer to assist me with the many chores, cooking, and cleaning.

There was always a lot of fun involved, too, and what a story they had to tell afterwards of the many people they met and activities in which they participated. This was also true for a few young men we hosted over the years who came north to learn about the Arctic and wilderness life.

People have often asked us why we live in such a remote place. "You must not like people," some said. But that is far from the truth. We love visitors! We tell people who make these observations, "We live here because our parents brought us here and we grew up loving our homeland!"

Yes, this remote life can be harsh, and we are totally dependent on our own abilities and industriousness, but the rewards of an independence and unique life are worth it.

*Teena and childhood friend
Doreen (Nutaaq) Simmonds
by Museum sign.*

Our Museum

Browsing the Golden Plover Museum is a fascinating part of any visitor's time at Colville Village. The museum's beginnings can be traced to a young boy's insatiable appetite for collecting samples of nature's bountiful treasures. Jim, and later all the family members, developed a propensity for saving interesting keepsakes collected in the Arctic: ancient bones and tusks, shells, artifacts, plants, mounted birds and animals. Many Iñupiat-made items, plus the Helmericks own Alaskan fur clothing and cold-weather paraphernalia are displayed in the museum.

Not only does the museum have a large collection of Alaskan items, but also various things from all over the world. Much of this was acquired by Jim's parents during extensive travels. Other people have also contributed items over the years.

Our son Derek mounted hundreds of life-like bird displays and made many study-skins of both birds and small mammals. Isaac also contributed mounted specimens to this outstanding collection. A person could spend many hours looking at the hundreds of objects in the museum. Visitors exclaim that every time they have returned, they have seen many new things they missed the earlier time.

Golden Plover Museum, corner of main museum room with many items including a manikin dressed in old caribou-fur clothing.

Greatroom in upstairs of lodge showing caribou mounts, many plants, and display cases in the lounge area. Teena's special sculptured wainscoting along west-facing outer wall.

One corner of main museum room where there are hundreds of mounted birds and specimens of all kinds.

West corner of Greatroom. The door goes into an eight by sixteen sunroom full of plants.

Upper NE wall in Greatroom with more mounts above our hibiscus tree.

One museum room is full of flying birds mounted by Derek.

Chapter 7
Pets and Animals at our Homesite

Pets

We have had many pets from the ordinary dogs, cats, parakeets, and gerbils, to the unusual box turtle, lemmings, and a little Savanna sparrow. We have raised many small farm critters like dairy goats, rabbits, chickens, ducks, and geese.

Dogs are probably the most common pet, especially for farms or remote homesites. We have had both work dogs and ones who were strictly pets. Prior to snowmachines becoming commonplace, sled-dogs were used for transportation for those of us living in Alaska, and we had working dogs for a dog-team for many years. Jim raised three pups for a three-dog team as a boy, and later in the 1970s, we had more than twenty dogs used for several teams. These were just traditional Iñupiat dogs to which we also bred a full-blood St. Bernard

Derek with two of our dairy goats that provided all the fresh milk we could use. Occasionally, we had enough milk and fresh eggs to share with our field-camp crews. Derek and Jay playing with their rabbits in 1977.

into the mix to increase the size and strength of dog, since our dogs were for freighting, not racing. They were used to haul firewood, buckets of water, chunks of ice to melt for water, whatever needed to be moved. A good lead dog that followed commands well was especially important in wide-open prairie country since there were no trails through the woods to follow, but just open snow-covered tundra or river/ocean ice.

After the Sea Mammal's Act of 1972 was passed and guides could no longer use airplanes in the hunting of polar bears, there was hope that we could still hunt out on the ice using dog-teams for transportation. Later, when polar bear hunting was never reopened except for Iñupiat, we sold or gave away most of our working dogs. Snowmachines were taking over the working dog's role and they didn't need daily care and food.

Finally, in the early 1980s, we no longer kept any sled-dogs, but had one or two dogs as house pets. Not only do dogs make great companions, but we found it important to have them as an alert mechanism. No animal or person could arrive at our place without us being alerted to their presence by a barking dog. Day or night, not a person, bear, fox, or even raven could sneak up on us. Several of our beloved dogs were a female Blue Heeler named Nico, a huge male Chesapeake Bay Retriever named Toby, and a beautiful golden Great Pyrenees named Ruby. These were great watch dogs and took their job very seriously of protecting their area from any object that invaded their space. Even an airplane or disliked predator bird flying over was announced.

Jim pumping fuel with his faithful Ruby by his side.

Clyde, the Caribou

We have had many pets that we rescued from the wild as orphans that we took in to raise and then return to the wild. This is especially true during the summer family-building season when all the wildlife around us are busy raising babies. One such baby was a little caribou calf that had been separated from its mother—this happens all too often.

He was just a lost little caribou about two months old. The kids first spotted him wandering around some of the out-buildings a couple of days after a large herd of caribou had stampeded across our island driven by the July bugs that plague them mercilessly. The calf stood about two feet at the shoulders and had a soft, light brown coat typical of baby caribou. He must have missed his mother's milk but seemed to be getting enough nutrition from the green grasses and lichen around the buildings.

He was good at evading the kid's attempts to get close to him. But gradually he became more and more accustomed to the presence of people walking around and shied away less often. We named him Clyde. It was always fun to see him around each day. Once, the boys tried to catch him by covering themselves with caribou hides and crawling up to him. It didn't work. Not fooled, Clyde pranced off as soon as they got close.

Summer ended. Clyde remained. He continued feeding among the many families of wild Brant, ptarmigan, and other birds that had raised their families on our island. The many young birds were testing and strengthening their wings and learning the layout of their birth area from the air so they would know where to return in later years.

For many years, we have kept a few dishes of wild bird feed out and about the area around our home as treats for the many birds that are such an important part of our summers. Since Clyde wandered around in the vicinity of several of these feed stations daily, his curiosity became peaked, and we noticed him sniffing around the dishes occasionally. Next thing we knew, he was eating the bird-treat crumbles like a kid who had just discovered candy. From then on, he would finish off any food left by the birds.

After freeze-up, when all the migrating birds had left, we continued putting a little food in one dish just for Clyde. We could nearly walk up to within touching distance of him by then as he had become so used to us. Soon he learned to wait at the dish in the morning when he knew we would be putting food in the dish on our way back from barn chores. One day, my husband Jim reached out and petted him while Clyde was busy munching down his morning treat. It didn't take long before Clyde would allow any of us in the family to touch him.

We kept expecting him to leave, since walking off the island was only a matter of crossing the frozen river now. Occasionally other caribou wandered onto the island. We thought Clyde would leave with them. Although he wandered around with them, when they left the island, he always returned. He would feed as much as several miles away from our buildings, but often returned here to lie down and chew his cud. We were able to observe his daily patterns of feeding and processing his food, along with leaving plenty of pellets around the yard.

By fall, Clyde had shed his baby coat and grown his adult coat of gray, white, and dark brown colors. He began growing his antlers, which started out as little buds, and then grew straight up about four inches. They remained covered with a thin coating of brown fur, similar to what is called velvet on big caribou. These little antlers would fall off by mid-winter, so he could begin to grow new ones in the spring as all male caribou do each year.

As winter progressed, we could look outside and find Clyde at any time, either out feeding or somewhere near the house, depending on time of day. He learned to lie down in the spots best sheltered from the wind, depending on which direction the wind was blowing. Wind is almost a sure thing on the arctic prairie.

Caribou are smart. Clyde soon learned our routines, and often waited at the door when he knew we came out for daily chores or other activities. He loved to join in with any activities such as wood cutting chores, hauling water, or walks to the

Clyde looking in kitchen window and chewing his cud while lying on the deck.

barn where we had small farm animals needing care. He reminded us of a dog, or other domestic animals we've had that insisted on being a part of whatever activity in which we were involved.

Clyde would stand next to the sawhorse right in the way as our son Isaac would cut firewood with the bow saw. He would run alongside the snowmachine as buckets of water were hauled on the trailing sled up to the house from our lake. Sticking his nose down in a bucket of water, he would raise his head snorting and shaking water from side to side.

Sometimes he became such a nuisance, he needed to be shooed away. One day Clyde had us all in stitches as we watched him push an empty five-gallon bucket around the yard. It rolled along in front of his nose like a ball and kept him entertained for half an hour before he tired of the game.

Clyde proved he had an excellent sense of smell in many ways. He discovered I kept a variety of frozen food stored outdoors near our back porch. Unless I kept my frozen bread products inside a wooden storage box, Clyde would sniff out the stuff and help himself to packages of hamburger buns or other food which he found desirable. Another example of Clyde's excellent smell was when Isaac was walking around on the tundra with Clyde one day and just for fun started digging around in the snow to uncover grass for Clyde to eat. What Isaac uncovered looked similar to areas that Clyde uncovered with his own hooves (shaped and used as excellent little shovels), yet Clyde would sniff at the area Isaac uncovered, reject it, walk a short distance with his nose to the ground, stop and dig, and then begin eating on some choice morsels he had uncovered. His nose could find exactly what he wanted to eat, even when it was covered by several inches of snow.

Clyde developed one unusual habit for a caribou that at first had me worried. Because of our family's commercial fishery in the early winter, by late fall we were occupied with handling all the fish that are caught, stored and packaged at our place. Clyde had many opportunities to sniff and investigate this product and he was soon tasting and nibbling on frozen fish scraps. Next thing we knew, he was chewing or sucking on the ends of whole fish. He would pull the fish meat right out of its skin as he ate it. This progressed to the consumption of several fish a day. I worried about what this would do to the digestive tract of an herbivore and voiced these concerns to my husband. He assured me that there was no need for alarm and told me about mules being fed dried fish during lean winter months, and other situations where herbivores ate something other than plants. Although Clyde liked his occasional fish or pelletized treats, his main diet stayed the wild prairie grasses for which he forged during much of every day.

We discovered that caribou make a number of vocalizations. The most obvious was a snort, soft and purr-like when he was contented, loud and obnoxious when he was disturbed. One day I kept hearing this sound that perplexed me, until I discovered it was coming from just outside the kitchen window. Snow had built up on our deck outside the window and Clyde was able to stand on the deck and look directly through the window into the house. He stood there, with his nose nearly touching the glass, snorting his displeasure that Isaac had left him to come indoors. They had been playing together earlier, which Clyde seemed to greatly enjoy. This little habit of coming to the window became routine whenever Clyde felt neglected.

A pet caribou or muskox was something we talked about occasionally, but never thought it would happen. Now that we had a pet caribou, we began to feel responsible for him.

Fate had brought him to us, and our befriending this wild creature and encouraging his presence with treats and our companionship had now put us in a position of responsibility. What would we do with him? Could he continue to live around our place?

As a new summer approached, we began thinking about the consequences of having a free roaming caribou around the place on a regular basis—a caribou that wasn't afraid to butt his way into any activity and had a super nose for sniffing out delectable food sources. As the wild birds returned from their winter migration south, we would be setting up several feed stations as we do every summer. Our own hand-raised waterfowl and livestock would be coming out of the winter barn to resume their life in the summer outdoor pens. Clyde would wreak havoc on the feed stations, and fences would be unable to stop him from doing the same to the feed dishes inside the pens.

After discussing various options, we decided we had to persuade Clyde to leave and take up a true caribou lifestyle of roaming great distances across the arctic prairie with others of his kind. We waited until mid-May, when the flooding of the river was imminent, and walked Clyde across the river ice from our island homesite to the mainland side of the river. Clyde had gone on walks with us before. We left a treat lying on the ground to occupy him while we hurried home. That was a futile attempt, as he was back at our sides before we could even reach the house.

Next, we used a snowmachine, which he followed obediently, both going, and unfortunately, returning. Our tactics needed more sophistication. Thus, we led Clyde far enough away to be way out of sight of our buildings, several miles to the east. We left some of his favorite treats scattered around in a lushly grassed area, and while Clyde was preoccupied eating, we drove away in the opposite direction of our place for many miles before doubling back in a very big loop. If Clyde followed the snowmachine trail that day, he got further and further away. That night the river flooded, and Clyde's sojourn at Colville Village ended.

There were other caribou in the area where we had left Clyde, so we hoped he would soon have companions of his own kind. We were able to watch these caribou meandering around with a spotting scope from the top floor of our two-story house for a number of days. It was difficult to be sure which caribou was Clyde though, because we had decided not to mark him in any way. We missed our friendly caribou, but there was no other workable choice open to us to ensure Clyde a future we considered acceptable. He was, after all, a wild creature, and deserved to have the freedom others of his kind had. We had experienced a rare treat of sharing in the life of this wild creature—one that left us with many fond memories.

Muskox Visitors

Another wild animal that spent time with us was the prehistoric-like muskoxen. A female muskox showed up unexpectedly in May 2010 during a spring blizzard. The wind was beginning to die down and we were scanning around the snowy landscape surrounding our homesite. We noticed an odd dark spot across the lake. Putting our spotting scope on the spot to identify what we were seeing, we were amazed that it was a muskox. It was lying down and we zoomed in on it and realized there was a second bump by its side. That immediately led us to believe she had a tiny calf.

As the storm abated, she began walking around feeding, and the little calf hugged her side. It was so tiny, we were convinced it was a newborn, brought into the world during the storm. The cow had found a small amount of shelter from the raging wind and blowing snow behind a big snowdrift on the far side of our lake. We had no idea from where she had come, although we knew there were several small muskoxen herds around the Sag and Kuparuk River Deltas, off to the east of us. For some reason, she had decided to wander many miles toward the west to give birth to her calf.

She stayed around on, or near, our land for many months—until the following fall. We were able to watch her little calf grow to half the size of his mother. We discovered it was a male calf.

They got used to our buildings and people walking around nearby, so we often enjoyed watching them munching the luscious tall grass and plants close to our house. They were wild animals and we

Muskox cow and calf graze by the house in July.

never wanted them to feel uncomfortable when nearby, so we always gave them plenty of space, plus kept our dogs inside if we saw them wandering close to our buildings. It was fun to have them around and we got many photos of them throughout that summer.

Come early fall, after freeze-up, she and the calf wandered off to the north and we did not see them again, although we eventually learned about her travels. During her stay with us, we discovered the cow was wearing a United States Fish and Wildlife Service (USFWS) tracking collar. Her naturally long hair hid it most of the time, but at one point when she was close to our house, we were able to read a number on her collar. After contacting the agency, we found out that the cow had been a part of the herd located on the Sag River prior to arriving at our place and later she returned to that herd with her half-grown calf. They had traveled many miles!

Another visitor was a muskox whose horns showed she was a three-year-old. Jim was outside cutting firewood when he looked upriver to see the muskox actually running down the frozen river toward our homesite. It was late October 2013, and she turned and ran up to one of our out-buildings and lay down to rest. Later, Jim was sorry he hadn't backtracked her trail to see if he could figure out why she was running as if being chased. We never found out.

We named her Missy, and she ended up staying around for most of the winter. Although she stayed a totally wild animal, she did become quite tame. Our dogs would run up and bark at her from a respectful distance, and she would sometime put her head down with a somewhat threatening stance, but usually she simply ignored them. The dogs were not brave enough to get too close. She fed all around on the island and often came up by the house to lie down or snoop curiously around. We had an old, oval wash tub by the back door to our house that irritated her for some reason, and she took to bashing it with her head every time she happened by it. She also used the corner of buildings to rub her head where her horns must have caused itching. She gradually let us approach her up to about ten to fifteen feet for pictures. Once Jim went outside the backdoor to face her head-on with his camera, but she was quite belligerent and tried to ram him with her horns. From then on, any idea of getting close enough to pet her was abandoned.

She did wander off a couple of times, but would eventually return until in late May, as spring break-up was upon us, she suddenly decided to leave at a run, just as she had arrived. It was strange, since she had nothing chasing her. It was as if the wanderlust hit her suddenly and she just had to go and go quickly. Off she ran toward the west across the flooding river delta channels, disappearing behind sand dunes on the horizon several miles away—still running. We never knew where she went, nor saw her again, but she had given us many months of enjoying one of nature's most amazing Arctic creatures. We hoped she had joined the small herd of muskoxen that usually hangs out about eighteen miles upriver from us, where they like to forge on the tall willow bushes along one of the tributaries to the Colville River.

Other Critters

Besides dogs and cats over the years, we had pet gerbils, ferrets, rabbits, and parakeets (budgies). The boys raised so many parakeets that they were selling young ones to some of the Fairbanks pet stores. Another small pet was the Greenland lemming, a small rodent related to mice and voles which lives on the Arctic tundra. We have two species: the Brown lemming which stays brown year-round and does not tame well, and the Greenland lemming, which turns completely white in the winter and does tame up well. These little balls of fur made excellent pets when gotten at a young age and took to cage life admirably, even using only one little spot for their toilet which made clean-up easy.

Orphans that we have taken in were many baby goslings over the years. Geese families negotiating the riverbanks often lost a baby who fell into a crack, or goslings got separated from parents during attacks from predators like a fox or an aerial hunter. We would have a hard time not rescuing a little one who was pitifully peeping from deep in a fissure in the bank. The parents would be long gone and despite other family groups around nearby, we almost never could get parent geese to accept a little lost gosling into their own family group. This meant we either had to desert it or take it home to raise ourselves. With no parent to protect it, many orphans became food for predators, but every summer, we ended up with a few orphans to feed and protect: baby White-fronted Geese, Brant, Snow Geese, Canada Geese, and even a few ducklings like Long-tailed Ducks. Since we did have domestic and exotic barnyard ducks and geese that we raised with our other small farm critters anyway, it was easy to incorporate a few extra babies into the menagerie, ones that eventually would be released back into the wild.

Barney

A little Brant gosling we named Barney was a very special example of one of our hand-raised wild babies. He was only a few days old when we rescued him from a crack in the riverbank just down the island from our house. He was so tiny and vulnerable, we had to keep him mostly in the house for his early days. He had his own little place with down from old nests and a hot-water bottle to keep him warm. As he grew, we were able to put him outside for part of the day in a covered pen, so aerial predators could not dive down and grab him, like a jaeger, glaucous gull, or raven. He was cuddled and carried around to special spots of luscious grass especially liked by goslings. He thought we were his parents—his family. He did not like being out of our sight.

Barney playing soccer with the boys.

Barney grew rapidly as all babies must do here in the Arctic's short summer. The boys played with him. He followed them everywhere, peeping loudly if he felt he was getting left too far behind. By early September, he had grown out his wing feathers and started testing his new flying abilities. At first, he flew only short distances at low altitude. As his confidence and flight muscles strengthened, he began flying higher and further. But he always came home, even after getting more buddy-buddy with other wild Brant that lived in the area. Eventually, his migration instincts took over and he flew away with a flock headed south for the winter. We were sad to see him go but knew this was what he needed to do. We wished him safety for his long journey to winter grounds somewhere near Baja, Central America.

Barney helping Teena's dad work on the generator.

In mid-May of the next year, we were delighted to see him back. Although he had a special identifying band on his left leg, there was no doubt Barney was back home to his birthplace and family. As Brant were arriving at our island after their long migration back north, one goose landed in our yard, and came running up to the first person out the door to greet him. He was so excited to see us. As summer wore on, Barney joined in with any outdoor activity he could. For some reason, he loved pecking around the small, noisy, portable generator we used to run power tools, or anywhere we were working outside. It was comical when he ran back and forth with the boys as they played games like touch football or soccer. This went on all summer, including having Barney fly alongside our boat when we went boating. Barney migrated south again that fall as all the wild geese staged and left for their winter areas.

The next spring, we were in for quite a surprise. Barney turned out to be a girl! You see, it is nearly impossible to tell goose sexes apart by plumage. Only actions tell the real story as they mature. We had simply thought our little gosling was a male, but SHE proved otherwise when she returned the second spring with a mate. We had to change Barney to Barnette and then called her mate Barney.

As she ran up to the first person out the door to greet her, the second **Brant** hung back, obviously upset over what Barnette was doing. It took several weeks before the new Barney finally grew to accept his mate's strange friends. He never became quite as friendly, but he learned to like the treats we gave Barnette at our wild bird feeders and stopped shying away from us when we were outside near him and Barnette.

Soon the Brant couple got busy with their summer job of procreation, as all the other returning birds were doing. Barnette chose a nesting spot within a short distance from the house and Barney stood guard for the twenty-four-day incubation of the eight eggs in the nest. As soon as the goslings were hatched and ready to leave the nest, Barnette brought them to our backdoor to show them off. Over the rest of the summer, the family continued to stay close to the house as they fed and raised their brood until time to migrate south again arrived.

Barney and Barnette continued to raise new broods every summer for some time. They added dozens of young birds to the local population of hundreds of Brant that form the largest Pacific Brant colony on the North Slope of Alaska.

Finally, a year came when they didn't return. We were sad, but felt blessed to have experienced quite a few years of their antics. Had they hung out around other people in the winter? Did they fly over an area where hunting geese was legal? We did not know. Plus, we never banded their young, so had no way of knowing how many of the friendly Brant that lived on our island in the summers were some of their offspring.

Raising orphan birds or animals generally requires state or federal permits, which we maintained for years. These critters were always trained to survive and released into the wild. One year, we were even asked by federal wildlife agents to raise several dozen baby ducks and geese that were confiscated from a poacher trying to leave the state with illegally-collected live eggs and babies. It was a lot of work, but always enjoyable.

Goslings are relatively easy to raise because they live mostly on land and are grazers. We usually supplemented

Hundreds of birds nest around us and Brant are one of our favorites.

their natural food with a store-bought dried ration similar to commercial chicken feed. Not so easy were the various ducklings we raised, such as a baby Long-tailed Duck and eiders, since ducklings feed and live mostly on water. We had to teach them to eat bugs and also the dried food supplements we called crumbles from the surface of the water. Harder yet was keeping the little down-covered bodies dry and warm. This is a feat the mother duck does by simply brooding her young. The natural oil on the mother's feathers rubs off on the ducklings and they come out of the nest already well-oiled in order to stay dry immediately. Then as the ducklings grow, they learn to preen their feathers from their own oil gland at the base of their tails.

For orphans without the mother duck, we had to protect the little ducklings from hypothermia, since they needed to get in the water to learn to eat, yet would get soaking wet and water-logged without their mother's protective oils. We found no way to substitute the mother's natural protective oils. We had to protect our ducklings by only letting them in water briefly and then putting them under heat lamps to completely dry off between sessions in the water. After a few days, they learned to preen themselves, so they could stay dry in water on their own.

Meanwhile, we devised a system whereby little ducklings could come and go between the water and the dry, heated area by themselves. Using a big, galvanized tub tipped slightly on end, we had water only in the downward side, and a towel laying along the bottom of the tub above the water to make scurrying up to the upper dry end easy. At the upper end of the tub was clean bedding under a heat lamp that kept that whole area warm. Here the ducklings could dry out, sleep, and also practice the art of preening, something they instinctively knew how to do, but just needed a few days to figure it out. As the babies grew up, they graduated to outdoor pens, and then our big lake. They were given more and more freedom to roam and would eventually join their wild friends to migrate south.

Over the years, there were some failures and sad losses, but also many joyous successes of healthy birds released into the wild. We raised and released many goslings, eiders and other ducklings. One fun thing about this was that many of these birds returned to our land and lake each year. It was mostly the females with their chosen mates who returned, since it is the females that always return to their birthplace and their mates follow. As with Barnette, the females usually taught their mates to trust us.

Farm Animals

We had quite a few farm animals over the years our children remained at home. This venture was started because of our desire to have fresh milk and eggs in a land where fresh products like these are hard to come by.

We brought our first dairy goats north on our annual big cargo plane in 1973, a pregnant Alpine doe named Sally and a young Toggenburg buck we named Brownie. We bought them from a small farm in Fairbanks. Although the doe was supposed to be pregnant and kid within a month or so, thus bringing us fresh milk that first winter, it ended up being two more years before we realized the goal of fresh goat milk on the Colville. It turned out that she was not pregnant, but only very fat.

The young buck fulfilled his duties that fall, and the next winter Sally gave birth to triplets, two buck kids and one little doe. They were born at night, as most our kids were over the years, and when we checked on Sally in the morning, the little doe's ear-tips were frozen. The ear-tips eventually fell off, but the ears healed and she was fine otherwise. We brought all three kids in the house since there was no heat in the goathouse. We lost Sally shortly after that due to an illness and had to go another whole year before Pixie, our first little Colville-born doe, produced her first kids and subsequent fresh milk. From then on, we had fresh milk.

Pixie turned out to be an excellent producer and often gave us up to three-quarters gallon of milk each milking, twice a day. She had kidded every year for many years since goats need to be bred every year—freshening it's called. At one point, we were milking three does, and we provided fresh milk along with eggs to field camps for a few years. But usually, one milking doe was all we needed to supply sufficient fresh milk for the family. Extra kids born added to our meat supplies.

Our next farm additions were Leghorn laying chickens. We built a small coop and started with about ten hens and a rooster. They lived in an unheated coop and naturally grew amazing coats of thick feathers. We had to keep a small kerosene lamp burning in the coop for eight to twelve hours of each day during the dark winter days in order to keep the hens laying eggs. Otherwise, too many dark hours would stop them from producing eggs.

A few years later, other birds joined our barnyard critters. We ended up raising many kinds of domestic ducks, geese, and even Guinea Fowl. We added game birds just for fun: Bobwhite Quail, chukers, and pheasants. Soon exotic waterfowl joined our farm. These were birds we raised to sell to collectors worldwide with permits to own federally-protected wild waterfowl and to raise them for zoos or their own collection. We had gotten acquainted with these people because of clients who hired us to help them get eggs or newly hatched chicks out of the wild under special permits they had received.

Farm animals took a lot of care, especially in winter when water for them was carried by hand in five-gallon buckets to the barn. In 1978, we built a two-story barn to house the goats, chickens, and waterfowl all in their own stalls. Having them together helped conserve heat in an otherwise unheated building.

Teena and Derek after milking the goat.

Summers were easier when all the waterfowl were in outdoor pens and the goats spent their days outdoors. The birds had plenty of water, and the goats fed entirely on the prairie grasses and only the milking doe(s) received a grain treat while being milked. However, buying the commercial feed and straw for winter was expensive as was its transportation costs. Some years we supplemented the goats' winter feed by harvesting the local Arctophila grasses that grew at the lake's edges in late summer. It could be cut with a scythe and dried for later use, almost like harvesting and baling hay.

Another interesting help we had with our animals' care was unusual bedding options we sometimes had. In the oil field, products sometimes used "down-hole" during the drilling operations were shredded materials like ground-up nutshells or woodchips that usually came in forty-to-fifty-pound bags—whole pallets full of them. Sometimes these products were left over from an operation and were given to us. It made excellent stall bedding and cut our costs down on buying straw.

We eventually downsized our farm animals, after our children grew up and left home, until the barn eventually stood empty. Fresh products had become easier to get, plus the care and expense of these animals had become too burdensome for two aging parents.

Bear Encounters

Our family enjoyed watching many wild animals over the years like wolves, wolverines, foxes, Arctic ground squirrels, weasels, and even small rodents. The big mammals like bears were indeed the most exciting. Grizzlies were usually a big problem due to their marauding, destructive tendencies. They have been responsible for occasionally killing our farm stock plus extreme ransacking of buildings. Polar bears tended to be more respectful of our property, and rarely caused problems

Polar Bears

Polar bears are without a doubt the most majestic of all Arctic animals. Our lives on our island in the Colville River Delta about a mile from the Arctic Ocean has given us the privilege of many opportunities to experience their amazing lives, mostly in a positive way and once in a frightening way. Let me share with you a few of these stories.

Commercial fishing has been one of our primary means of livelihood, and the main fishing is done in October and November when nets are strung out under the ice to catch several varieties of whitefish, mainly Arctic Cisco and Least Cisco averaging one-half to one-quarter pound. The Arctic Cisco, locally known as Qaaqtaq, is our main cash crop and the Least Cisco is a secondary fish we sell as dog food. It is this time of year we are likely to see female polar bears who come in off the ocean ice to look for a maternity den site. One year we had an unforgettable encounter.

It was a very foggy morning, about -5°F and just starting to get light when Jim and Derek left to go pick nets out on the river ice. I listened to the sound of the snowmachine's engine fade away and glanced out the window to see them disappearing into the whiteness. I turned away from the window to get busy with the children's school lessons. Suddenly I became aware that the engine sound was getting louder again. Why were they coming back? That wasn't normal and I was anxious to find out what was going on. Jim and Derek soon walked through the doorway and with a purposeful march, they disappeared into different rooms and reappeared with camera gear in hand. Jim was slow to explain—he delighted in keeping us in suspense—but he finally told us that they saw something big out by our first net hole and he was pretty sure it was a bear, although it

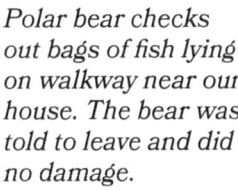

Polar bear checks out bags of fish lying on walkway near our house. The bear was told to leave and did no damage.

was hard to tell for sure because of the fog. They had decided to return to the house for cameras before continuing the rest of the way out to the net-picking site.

The fog was starting to lift slightly and as I watched the snowmachine, sled and two bundled figures fade again into the haze, I thought I could see a large shape out on the ice. The fog lifted more, and then I was sure it was a polar bear for it stood up and took several steps. Its form was unmistakable. School was forgotten as the children and I crowded around the window facing the river to watch what would happen as Jim and Derek drove toward the bear.

They stopped a couple hundred yards away and I could see cameras coming out from inside their parkas and being pointed toward the bear. Slowly they walked toward the bear, getting closer and closer. The bear seemed unperturbed by the approach of the noisy snowmachine or the silent figures slowly moving nearer. I could tell the bear was occupied beside a large hump on the ice, which I figured was a pile of our fish that had been left on the ice from previous days' catches. Derek stayed back as Jim continued to walk closer to the bear. Derek later told me he hung back in apprehension yet continued to take pictures of his father approaching the bear closer and closer, and he certainly hoped none of his shots would be of a bear attacking his dad.

Polar bears often meander the coastline in fall and when they wander across our land, they rarely cause problems or stick around long. They are waiting to get back out on the ocean ice to hunt seals, their main diet.

It wasn't long before my husband and oldest son, whose proximity to the bear was beginning to make me uneasy, had jumped back on the snowmachine and were returning to the house. But their return was only to warm up frozen cameras and get more film. They were soon back, socializing with our visitor. Jim had told me it was a young female and she was busy eating fish, as I suspected. We assumed she had come off the ice to look for a den site, but for some reason was thin and hungry. Bears in the past had never stayed around long though, nor bothered any of our fish. This bear was apparently enjoying her feast of fresh-frozen fish and wasn't even distracted by the activity around her.

Not knowing how long she would stay, Jim was anxious to photograph her as much as possible. He was able to walk within forty or fifty feet of her before she showed any signs of being uneasy. The bear wandered around a little bit but never got far from the fish pile as she continued to eat.

Jim and Derek left and went to pick a different set of nets further down the river. They were sure the bear would be gone by the time they returned home for lunch, and then they could go pick the close-by nets after lunch. But surprisingly, she was not gone. Finally, Jim decided to go try and pick the nets despite the bear. This time they drove the snowmachine right up to the hole at which they needed to work. The bear had acted

Polar bear wandering in yard near deck and kitchen window.

reluctant to leave as they drove up, but she finally stood up and casually started away from the pile of fish. Suddenly she turned back and picked up one more fish and strolled away with it in her mouth as if to say, "Alright, if I must move, at least I'll take a fish to munch on." Bears have their dignity. Since there were four net holes with several more piles of fish, she moved over to a different pile of fish and again laid down to continue eating, holding each fish between her paws as she chewed.

Jim and Derek chopped open the first two frozen-over holes in the ice and pulled the net up on the ice to pick the fresh fish out of it. There were three nets to pick, and the bear was forced to move several more times before the nets were done. There were about a thousand fish total from this set of three nets when the picking was done and most of those fish were gathered up and brought back to the house to be packaged for market. The fish freeze immediately once out of the net, and they are later sold fresh-frozen. We transport the fish back to the warehouse in a large box that is tied onto the sled pulled behind the snowmachine.

Derek and Jim finished picking the nets and gathered the catch and came in off the ice for the day. The one variety of fish we catch to sell as dog food, Least Cisco, is often left out on the ice to be picked up at a later time, and it was these fish that the bear was rapidly consuming. We didn't expect to see her the next day though. Most bears that show up in the fall don't stay around long. Jim and Derek were both pleased with the pictures they had gotten.

Derek picking net with a feeding polar bear a short distance away.

The next morning, as daylight increased enough to see forms taking shape in the distance, we were all looking out the windows to see if we could spot the bear. Surprisingly, she was still there lying by the same net site. Jim and Derek had their cameras loaded again and off they went for their morning's fish picking. By the end of the second morning of sharing the ice with our furry visitor, Jim and Derek were getting less cautious and more at ease working next to their unusual companion.

In the afternoon, Jim took time off from the day's work to drive our three younger sons and me out on the ice near the bear so we could get a closer look at her. Looking with binoculars from the windows wasn't nearly as exciting as actually seeing her standing only a mere hundred feet away. As we watched, she walked off and, using her paws, dug herself a bed in the soft snow along the riverbank. She stretched out to sleep off a belly full of fish. She was just below the bank that was almost exactly opposite from the bank our house stood on.

By the third day, the bear's presence seemed almost commonplace. She would barely move fifty to a hundred feet away as the guys worked the nets. Two white foxes ran about getting their share of fish, timid, yet brave enough to grab a fish and dash off to bury it for later. Bears and foxes are well accustomed to each other since they are frequent traveling companions. Jim forgot to remove the better fish from the ice after picking the first net and the bear came over and ate up most of the fresh fish as soon as they had moved on to the next net. Now she knew which fish were the fatter-and-better-tasting ones. It was like replacing lean rabbit with bacon. Jim was kicking himself for not getting our better fish safely put in the transporting box. He and Derek quickly remedied that mistake on the next net and picked up the Qaaqtaq and put them in the box on the snowmachine sled. But Mrs. Bear learned quickly and as soon as Jim and Derek moved on to the last net, she followed her nose quickly over to the box and began battering it around until she knocked a piece of the plywood side off and stuck her head in to begin the feast. Jim decided it was time to let Mrs. Bear know her limits. He started walking toward her telling her in a gruff voice to back off and leave our box alone. She seemed to know she had stepped out-of-bounds, and she turned and walked back to the pile of less desirable fish, the Least Cisco. Jim continued to leave plenty of fish on the ice for her and by now she had eaten at least two hundred pounds.

Before returning home that day, they watched Mrs. Bear perform quite a comical feat. She walked over to one of the net holes and looked at the piece of plywood lying over the hole to keep the ice from freezing too thick. With dexterity, she carefully lifted the plywood with one paw and while holding it up, she took a drink. Then she gingerly set the plywood back down exactly as it had been. She seemed to be showing them that she could be careful if she wanted.

When Jim and Derek came in off the ice for lunch, the bear wandered over toward the house and walked up around our various buildings. She only looked around a bit and left again which was quite a relief. However, later she returned after Jim and Derek had gone back to work at the second net site down-river. Jay, our eleven-year-old, had gone out to saw firewood when I looked out the window and saw Mrs. Bear walking toward our warehouse only a hundred feet away. I quickly stepped out on the porch and called Jay to come back in the house. I kept my voice calm but couldn't help but be apprehensive, knowing bears can be unpredictable. Mrs. Bear had proved herself to be calm and unaggressive out on the ice around the fellows, but now she was in new territory, and I wasn't sure what she would do.

Predictably, she followed her nose to the morning's fresh fish still lying out near the warehouse. She wreaked havoc among the neatly laid out fish, not really eating much, but taking bites here and there, mangling many of them. I knew Jim would be angry. I stepped out on the porch and yelled at her to get away from our fish. She looked over at me as if to say, "Ah, Ma." I watched her wander off, but she didn't go far.

Polar bear strolling by our parked plane with several older homesite buildings behind him.

"Bruno," who hung around for seventeen days, is lying on porch under my kitchen window by my flower planter.

The next thing I knew she was walking toward our frantically barking sled-dogs tied fairly close to our back porch. She ignored the dogs and walked right over to the porch and put one foot on the first step. Our outside door has a window in it, and I was just inside on the porch behind the window. With a racing heart, I again spoke harshly to the bear. She looked up at me and then slowly backed away. There was no fear in her, only respect for what she knew was mine.

She walked about one hundred feet away and made herself a bed in the snow beside our warehouse and lay down to sleep. She had pushed up a clump of snow into a nice pillow and then rested her head on one paw before settling down. There she stayed. I was relieved she was causing no more worries for the time being. I gave Jay the go ahead to go back to his wood cutting chores.

When Jim and Derek returned on the snowmachine from picking the far nets, they could tell at once by the scattered fish that the bear had been up by the house and causing trouble. Just then she awoke, jumped up, and started to run off. Jim decided it was time to encourage her to be on her way elsewhere. He chased after her with the snowmachine and kept her running for several miles, hoping she would get the idea that she had worn out her welcome. We were all sad to see her go, but then again, we were afraid to let her stay around and get in serious trouble or continue to get too familiar with people.

She never did return around the buildings again, although she did return to the fishing holes occasionally over the next week before leaving the area for good. Our special visitor had consumed nearly a thousand pounds of fish during her stay with us. We were glad to be able to share our fish with her and help ensure the months ahead in her den would be successful ones. She had unknowingly shared with us, too, just by giving us the opportunity and pleasure of being able to watch one of the Arctic's most magnificent creatures.

Polar bears have wandered by our place numerous times, but another polar bear visit that lasted for an enjoyable seventeen-day visit was the fall of 1999. It was September 1, and the grass was still green around the house. We looked out the kitchen window to see a young male bear, perhaps five or six years old, walking along our deck. It seemed strange to see a polar bear when there wasn't even any snow on the ground. He appeared quite thin and lethargic, and we later realized he must have been this way due to time of year and little food— perhaps a natural way to preserve energy.

After wandering around the house and nearby buildings, he ambled over and lay down on a big straw pile by our now-empty barn, about two hundred yards from our house. Over the days he stayed on our land, this became his special spot. We had to look around to find where he was before going outside, especially to walk our house dog on the opposite side of the house from him. We named the bear Bruno and took many pictures of him.

He minded his own business, and we gave him a respectable space although outside chores still needed to be done. We kept a close eye on him, but Bruno ignored the people he saw walking around cutting firewood or other chores. He usually slept the day away at his spot by the barn and did his wandering at night. Some days we woke to soft feet padding along the deck just outside our bedroom window, but he quickly left when he heard noises inside the house. One morning I took pictures of him snacking on dead flowers in one of my flowerpots below my kitchen window.

What kept Bruno here was an old fish pile we had buried for fertilizer on one corner of our property. He had sniffed it out, dug it up, and ate on the rotten pile until his lethargy faded away. He became more active, but still remained mannerly. It was fun to watch him go for a swim in our lake.

After about sixteen days with us, Bruno suddenly jumped up with his nose in the air and headed resolutely north toward the ocean pack-ice. We watched him disappear over the sandbars separating our island from the ocean. The next day he was back. Hmm, maybe he was reluctant to leave, but soon he lifted his nose to the northern sky and struck out again. This time he never returned, and the call of the wild ocean ice won out. He had stayed with us for seventeen days. One disagreeable outcome of Bruno's visit was many extremely stinky bear poop-patties that had to be cleaned up around the yard, since our dog discovered they were wonderful to roll in to cover himself with great smells! How disgusting is that!

This fall-time bear scenario has happened again several times, although none of these later bear episodes had the bear sticking around more than a day or two. One bear lingered a few days because of the remains of a caribou carcass nearby from a summer kill. When this was consumed, he left.

The last story of a polar bear is one I really don't like to tell, because I always took pride in being able to answer people's questions about living around dangerous bears with the statement, "We have never feared bears, nor had any problems with them!" But the following story was an anomaly and not the bear's fault, plus it has a sad ending.

Teena's Unfortunate Encounter

I mixed up ice-cream sugar-milk mix after dinner. Toby, our large Chesapeake Retriever, was nervous and wanted outside, so I let him out ahead of me. I normally never let him go with me when I'm getting snow mixed in ice-cream mix so he won't get around the clean snow I find to use. Praise God, I didn't think of that this time, only that he was impatient to be let out.

I walked out looking around for some soft, clean snow deep enough to scoop up into my bowl. There was a small mound of snow beside the wood pile Aaron had stacked up earlier in the fall just NE of the garage. I walked over there and was just leaning down to start scooping snow when I looked up and a small polar bear was charging toward me, coming from the direction of the river porch in the southwest. At once, I recognized it as a large cub. (Jim thinks it was probably at least a two-year-old.) It was still big enough to stop my heart as it charged me! I don't know if I screamed at that point—I don't remember saying any words—just instant thoughts that a BIG mamma bear had to be right behind this small bear.

I took steps backwards and the bear came on lunging toward me. I threw the whole bowl, bowl contents, and large spoon at the bear's face as he grabbed for me. I saw the sugary milk splash all over his face, top of his head, and neck. That stopped him momentarily and he turned to look at the bowl hitting the ground to his one side but was turning back toward me just as

Teena and Toby, the hero dog.

Toby came around the inside corner of the woodpile barking and snarling ferociously. The bear turned away from me and I ran around the back of the garage and powerhouse, pausing to look carefully around the building, still expecting to see a bigger mamma bear.

The way was clear, so I dashed to the front corner of the powerhouse, paused to look again and seeing no threat, I ran to the house, and practically crawled up the steps in a panic. Toby's barks and growls continued ferociously indicating a fierce fight, but I didn't turn to look, nor could I have seen them, since the fight had moved closer to the riverbank and was hidden by the garage.

I ran in the house screaming (literally "bloody murder," as the saying goes) Jim's name, and he came out of the sitting room wondering what was going on. I screamed that a polar bear had Toby, and that Toby had just saved my life—go help him!!!

Jim told me to keep calling Toby back to the house, which I did desperately from the porch doorway.

A shotgun was not on the porch like usual and Jim hesitated as to the quickest action to take. He then remembered the shotgun just inside the powerhouse door and ran for it. He was frantically trying to get the shotgun to load—there was a slight jamming problem—as he ran around the corner of the garage. Jim said at that point he saw Toby's woefully begging eyes looking at him from under the bear who had Toby pinned down with its jaws clamped on the top of Toby's neck. Toby was no longer barking and pretty helpless at that point. Perhaps he had turned his back on the bear to run toward my calling voice and the bear pounced on his back. We don't know since we hadn't been able to see the fight.

Jim then leveled the gun and shot the bear broadside and high, trying not to hit Toby. The bear was thrown sideways, releasing Toby, who ran to Jim. Toby started to run back toward the bear again when Jim shot again and the bear collapsed. Jim brought Toby to the house and found fresh ammo and got outdoor gear on to go back out. There was still the strong possibility of another bear nearby. He first confirmed that the young bear was dead—Yes. Then he carefully walked around looking for other tracks or evidence indicating from where the cub had come.

Tracks showed it was only one bear and he'd been around looking for food for a while even dragging a muskox skull off the bench on the deck. How he could do that without us hearing or seeing it was amazing. Perhaps Toby had been hearing something which is what had made him nervous and wanting out. We've had foxes all around since freeze-up and Toby has barked a lot over them, both from inside and outside the house. So, I'm still puzzled why Toby didn't indicate by barking about any sounds the bear must have been making earlier. TV noise probably disguised it, is my guess.

Anyway, tracks showed the single bear had followed Jim and Toby's tracks down the riverbank from the northeast as they returned earlier in the day from walking over to close the big hanger doors. The bear seemed too young to be on its own so has been separated from its mother for whatever reason? Perhaps she was killed? We left the bear lie where it fell for the night (it was nearly dark by then and we still didn't know if another bear would show up), but we reported to U.S. Department of Fish and Wildlife. They have no problem with the kill in defense of life, and plan to come retrieve the hide and skull as soon as weather permited. It is snowing and blowing now.

We skinned the bear this morning. It wasn't much larger than Toby lengthwise, but weighed much more than Toby—a BIG roly-poly cub. It wasn't starving yet. The fat still on it had turned pink like it was being reabsorbed, which indicates the cub must have been on its own and gone without food for quite some time. If it had been an experienced killer, Toby wouldn't have stood a chance.

Just writing about the encounter has my stomach tied in knots. I hardly slept at all during the night. I couldn't stop thinking about the what ifs, like what if I hadn't let Toby out with me, or what if there had been a mother bear around. We discovered by following his tracks, that Toby had gone straight out and picked up the bear's tracks around the warehouse. It was a northeast wind, so the smell of the tracks attracted Toby first while the bear itself must have been on or near the southwest side deck when we first went out (downwind for us, but not for the bear). Toby was just returning from over by the warehouse when he got to me just in time. Had he been a second later, I'm pretty sure the bear would have had me in his jaws.

Well, I've reread Psalm 121:7-8 several times this morning: *The Lord will keep you from all harm—he will watch over your life; the Lord will watch over your coming and going both now and forevermore.*

By the way; more about Toby. His head and neck were all wet with bear slobbers and tufts of loose hair were all over, but no blood or wounds that we could find. Although the bear's teeth are full of Toby's hair, it seems that Toby's tough collar and thick hide and hair on the top of his neck protected him just long enough. Like I said, had it been an older bear, I'm sure that wouldn't have been the case. Toby's neck must be sore because he wouldn't let me try to clean off his neck last night. However, he rolled and rolled in the snow and let me rub snow into his hair this morning.

This episode certainly reinforces the need to be especially observant before venturing outside this time of year and take Toby with me!

This account of Teena's encounter with a polar bear on the evening of October 6, 2004, near her home on the Colville River Delta, was written the morning after the incident as a message to her family.

I must conclude this story with information we learned later to give background to this sad episode. A polar bear sow had been killed at Oliktok, about fourteen miles northeast of our land. Two large cubs had been with her and they wandered off without "Mom" to become lost and hungry, not yet able to survive alone. One cub was later seen further down the coast to the east. The other cub was the poor, starving cub that tried to attack me in its desperate state. Regardless, it would have had little chance of surviving even if it had not ventured to our homesite.

Grizzly Bears

Grizzly bear stories often end badly for the bear or for whatever mess the bear leaves behind. Episodes usually involve broken-into buildings and sometimes dead farm animals. Grizzlies are usually ill-mannered and more aggressive than polar bears.

Grizzlies always have lived on the North Slope, but as a very small population, especially near the coast. However, the population exploded in the early days of the oil field

Grizzly bear on tundra near our home.

development due to sloppy handling of food wastes. It became a crisis in the 1980s and measures were taken to eliminate exposure to all food waste for predators like bears and foxes. Strict requirements were enforced for use of dumpsters with special lids to cover any wastes associated with food. This helped slow down the population explosion of those predators that had benefited from access to people food.

A special program was implemented to capture mischievous bears from the Prudhoe Bay area to release them to far away destinations. Some of these bears stayed away, some returned. A few bears that became dangerous had to be dispatched. As the easy food supply dried up around the oil field, some bears dispersed across the coastal area to become a source of problems wherever they went.

One detrimental effect was to the summer's nesting bird populations, since a grizzly bear could destroy a whole colony of nesting geese in one day of "fun-filled" marauding, eating a bit, but mostly just killing birds and destroying nests. Even with hunting permits increased to help reduce grizzly populations, those of us living on the North Slope have had to contend with this increase of bears. The same has been true with aerial predators such as Ravens and Glaucous Gulls. These predators are also devastating to nesting birds on the open tundra.

PART THREE

Along the Way of Our Arctic Life

Aerial of Anachlik Island looking north toward the Arctic Ocean during the winter months. The shadow of airplane can be seen below the buildings.

Chapter 8
Arctic Environment

It is common to break down a year into four seasons: winter, spring, summer, and fall. Therefore, I would like to describe our Arctic seasons for you as we have come to know them thoroughly over the many years of our lives here on the Colville River Delta. Our lifestyle becomes very cyclical based on the seasons and the routines and chores necessary for that time of year. This independent life can be harsh at times but does bring plentiful rewards if you are willing to wade through the challenges of hard work, weather hazards, and disappointing weather-related setbacks. We live here because we believe the joys of Arctic living outweigh the hardships.

Winter

Winters in the Arctic on the Colville are definitely harsh, and weather conditions make firewood and water chores associated with daily life the most challenging of the year. Not only do we have many weeks of well below zero temperatures, but the days of merciless winds, no daylight, and other hazards add an element rarely experienced in more southern regions.

Temperatures in the minus twenties Fahrenheit are common and can reach down into the minus fifties and even minus sixties occasionally. Our coldest day on record on Anachlik Island was -63°F in March 1986. Except for emergencies, our normal cut off for low-temperature travel is -30°F. Metal in equipment becomes almost like glass in extreme cold, and the danger of mechanical breakdown is increased exponentially.

One winter hazard is what is referred to as whiteout conditions. With snow-covered ground and an overcast sky, it all blends together into one solid white world. There is no horizon and no shadows to give visible depth perception. All you see in front of your eyes is white soup. If you have never experienced this phenomenon, let me give you some examples. Just to walk outside to dispose of a bag of garbage at our burn pile a few yards from the house means stumbling along as if blind. With no shadows to guide you, your eyes have no way to see the ups and downs of the ground in front of you. You take a few steps and suddenly you step off a drop-off in the snowdrift on which you are walking and down you go. Pick yourself up and try another few steps, suddenly you walk into a wall of snow, an incline you had no idea was there. Step by step is the same. You carefully navigate, testing each step. Coming back to the house is no better for you can't even see the steps you just made in the snow moments before. Walking or even driving a snowmachine in whiteout conditions is quite a dangerous proposition. Yet working and moving around outside is a necessity that cannot always be avoided, no matter what the weather conditions are.

On top of cold temperatures and whiteout conditions, it is a land of frequent and persistent winds. Our yearly average wind speed is eleven mph. Blizzards can rage for days or even weeks on end from thirty up to sixty mph. We have even had storms with winds in the sixties, gusting to one hundred mph speeds, although these are very rare. Frequent windstorms create blizzards that can obscure visibility to only a few feet, making

Modern GPS helps Jay and Isaac find their way home in whiteout conditions.

travel impossible and outdoor work miserable. Because the Arctic prairie is a desert by precipitation standards, out on the flat tundra, the ground and grasses often can still be seen sticking up through the snow all winter—the snow that does lay on the ground is just blown back and forth all winter by the changing winds. It forms hard longitudinal drifts that run the direction of the prevailing northeast and southwest wind directions. Larger drifts are beat into hard-packed mounds that surround any obstacle that breaks the wind, big things like our buildings down to little things like a simple wooden stake in the ground. These large snowdrifts must be negotiated over— up, down, and around—when walking or driving a vehicle around the buildings. Some are as high as ten to fifteen feet and stretch out many yards long and ten to fifteen feet thick, creating serious obstacles for anyone moving around outside.

Another consequence of living in this windy land is windchill, a phenomenon that is created when wind speed makes cold air temperatures feel colder. When wind is added to cold air, exposed flesh will freeze much more quickly than in still air. There are very few days here along Alaska's northern coast that are wind free, and this added windchill factor to cold endurance makes how we dress for this cold very important.

High winds carve sastrugi (waves of large snow drifts) on the landscape.

High winds create huge drifts around the buildings that have to be shoveled out. The drift here is over fifteen feet high. The boys would dig snow caves in the drifts.

Add a twenty mph wind to -20°F and it becomes -48°F Exposed flesh will freeze within minutes. It is because of this windchill factor that native peoples of northern climates learned to protect their faces with fur ruffs. The ruff directly around and slightly forward of the face is imperative. It creates an insulating air pocket or barrier between the skin and extreme cold.

Our family has used fur outer garments as our Iñupiat friends do, and I learned to sew fur clothing for all my family. Fur parkas, mukluks and mittens were "old hat" for me anyway, having worn them as a child in Barrow. Wolf, wolverine, and

Southwest end of house/lodge just after a fierce winter storm coming out of the northeast. Snow was driven into drifts that covered the first story windows and was beaten into siding, along window frames, and packed into the antenna tower.

Colville Village Sun Chart
Latitude: 70° 25'   Longitude: 150° 24'

	Sun First Up	Sun Up for 12 Hours	Sun Up for 24 Hours	Sun First Down	Sun Down 12 Hours	Sun Down 24 Hours
Jan	Jan. 18					
Feb						
Mar		Mar. 20				
Apr						
May			May 15			
June						
July				July 29		
August						
Sept					Sept. 23	
Oct						
Nov						Nov. 24
Dec						

Dates vary several days depending on the year.
Total number of days sun never sets = 75
Total number of days sun never rises = 56

The sun rises for the first time each year about January 18. At first it only tops the horizon in the southern sky and sets again shortly. Each day it stays up longer and climbs a little higher in the sky. The distance between where it rises and sets along the horizon expands each day; its point of rising moves toward the east and it sets more toward the west.

By March 20, the sun is above the horizon for twelve hours a day, and it spans half the distance around the horizon. It makes a low arc in the sky from sunrise to sunset, with the pinnacle of the arc directly south and only about halfway up in the sky. The sun never reaches directly overhead in the Arctic.

By May 15, the sun no longer sets. It merely circles around the horizon, reaching its highest point directly south and its lowest point directly north. Picture a tilted circle compared to the flat circle of the horizon.

On July 29, the sun first begins to set again. It now reverses the order it started in January, and slowly decreases the time it remains above the horizon and its movements around the horizon.

By September 23, the sun's time above and below the horizon is equal—twelve hours. The sun sets its final time for the year on November 24. The sun is not seen again until January 18 of the next year.

fox are the common fur for ruffs. Caribou, wolf, and seal fur are most common for parkas, pants, or mukluks. Martin and Arctic ground squirrel fur are favorites for dress parkas. Although caribou hides are still the warmest and lightest fur for garments, since caribou hair is hollow and brittle, it breaks and sheds badly, so it has often been replaced in modern days mostly by store-bought sheep hides. This fur makes very warm garments, but they are considerably heavier than those made with caribou hides. Rabbit fur is occasionally used.

Back to conditions that greatly affect our Arctic lives. On top of cold temperatures, whiteouts, winds, and windchill, winter brings long days of darkness. There is no doubt that these dark days in winter are challenging, and this lack of sun is much of the essence of the Arctic. Any area above the Arctic Circle experiences one or more days where the earth's axis is tipped away from the sun such that no sun is seen above the horizon at all. When a person asks what the Arctic Circle is, I explain that it is the most northern parallel of latitude that runs north of the equator at 66° 30' N. Everything north of this invisible line is the Arctic where the sun is above the horizon for twenty-four continuous hours at least once per year and below the horizon for twenty-four continuous hours at least once per year. The further north one travels from this Arctic Circle line, the number of sunless or sunlit days increase.

Spectacular aurora filling the sky on clear nights are common, ground lights from Kuparuk are in the background.

Amazing halos, perihelia and rare patterns form around the sun at Colville.

Here at our Colville home, the days where no sun is ever above the horizon fluctuates between fifty-six and fifty-seven days. These dark days are never complete darkness for twenty-four hours a day. The retreat of the sun in early winter and its return in late winter happens gradually. There is always a varying period of twilight mid-day when the upper rim of the sun reaches the closest proximity to our horizon. So, the idea of total darkness twenty-four hours a day for weeks on end in the winter is really not true. Here in the far north, the sun's arc gets lower and lower in the sky each day as fall progresses, and on November 24 the sun drops below the southern horizon for the final time of that year, not to be seen again until January 18 of the next year. These many days of low or no sun does add

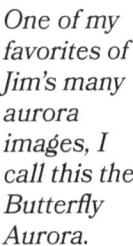

One of my favorites of Jim's many aurora images, I call this the Butterfly Aurora.

an element of harshness to life that only Arctic dwellers fully experience. Yes, it is the low point of our Arctic year.

In my early years on the Colville, before we could afford continuous electricity in winter, the dark days had much more effect on our lives. Our light consisted mainly of kerosene or gas lamps, and even school lessons were conducted around one table with only one gas lantern burning to light the room. Our boys thought it was comical when they read in schoolbooks about ancestors using oil lamps, when they were used to them in their present days.

In more recent years, we began running a small generator twenty-four hours a day during the coldest, dark days and the bright lights in the house and yard help dispel the effects of light depravity. December falls right in the middle of these dark days, and we only have a few hours mid-day with twilight, where outdoor chores can be completed without extra light. Even with good sources of light indoors, these low-light days affect our daily lives by reducing our energy levels and requiring extra sleep. As the sunshine and daylight increase and winter wanes, our energy levels begin to increase again, and less sleep is needed.

Even with the sun rising again, February is usually our coldest month of the year, with minus twenties to thirties degrees Fahrenheit the norm. We occasionally see minus forties and fifties degrees Fahrenheit, too. Even March can be quite cold. Our coldest ever, -63°F, was recorded on the Colville homesite in March. However, the returning sun still makes it seem as if spring is right around the corner.

There is so much natural beauty to winter in the Arctic, despite its hardships. The Aurora Borealis is undoubtedly the most impressive. Although the northern lights are shining year-round, during the darker days of winter is when we get the show. We can't see them during our increased daylight seasons. The colors, movement, and amazing expanse of sky filled with dancing lights are breathtaking. It is never the same, and always awe inspiring. Jim has incredible pictures of the Aurora Borealis as regularly seen from our home on clear nights.

Light Pillars rise high into the sky.

Another winter phenomenon is the bright moon reflecting on the great expanses of snow. You can even read by the moonlight it is so bright. Yet another atmospheric phenomenon we see in our cold air conditions is the formation of ice crystals that produce beautiful halos, perihelia (moon and sundogs) and other rainbow-like arc patterns around the moon and sun. These are unique to cold climates where ice crystals can form.

Probably the most unusual atmospheric phenomenon we experience are incredible mirages. Mirages are images of real objects that have been displaced by light being bent due to thermal gradients. The object, which may be totally out of view under normal air conditions, can suddenly appear in the distance in front of you. Made by reflected light from the real object, the mirage is a mirror image or inverted. Sometimes

Mirage of oil facility as seen east of our homesite. With no mirage, the ground level view with bare eyes from six miles away would see no structures, yet with the mirage, the rig and buildings are clearly seen.

there are multiple layers of the image, alternating between erect and inverted, but stacked directly above the real object, and even below the real object occasionally. This optical phenomenon can cause what looks like entire cities to appear on the horizon—such as when we look toward oil company infrastructure centers. A mirage can raise towers of lights in the dark hours, or strange images in daylight, of unbelievable structures in the sky, such as rows and rows of lights or objects waving on the horizon. But they are actually distant objects, not even visible under normal conditions. Light Pillars are refracted light phenomenon due to ice crystals in cold air. These are amazing columns of light that rise high into the sky above real ground lights.

The snow itself is capable of great beauty. Snow is shallow on the open tundra because this is a desert; only small amounts of precipitation fall. Little tufts of prairie grass poke up through the snow, and frost can make the seed-heads look like miniature trees. Sometimes the snow sparkles like fields of diamonds by the millions. When ice crystals fall from the sunny sky, the flakes lie scattered on the ground like intricate lace, each flake distinguishable, unique, and beautiful. But where the persistent winds howl around obstacles, huge snow drifts can form and sometimes amazing formations like sastrugi can be carved into hard, rippling waves suspended in time. Imagine driving a snowmachine through terrain like waves of hard cement.

When the sun is low in the sky, as it is when it first returns from its sleep below the horizon, it casts a blueish light that makes long, eerie shadows. Later, in the early spring, the sun reaches higher in the sky and makes the snow sparkle like diamonds. Walking among the brightly shining glitter is like walking in a fairy land.

Drive to Pingok Island

Isaac and I did a lot of cruising around on our snowmachines just for fun the winter of 1997. Since Isaac was our only son home at the time, we decided to go exploring on Sundays.

One Sunday close to spring we decided to check out some old, abandoned buildings along the shore east of Oliktok.

It was about 15°F with an eight mph breeze from the northeast. Isaac gassed up the two snowmachines; he drove his red snowmobile, and I drove the larger family work machine. We left at about 1:30 p.m. and started out, heading east. Driving overland was very rough going and we could only cruise along at a little less than twenty mph. (Isaac claims he usually goes much faster but was only going slow for my benefit.) Your body is constantly being jarred and it is strenuous on your muscles to hang on, steer, and keep the pressure on the throttle. It doesn't seem like much at first, but after hours of taken a beating like that, it is very tiring.

It was late spring, but terrain was still like winter, with lots of sunshine. Birds were just beginning to arrive north and as we reached the Kalubik Creek, we saw a pair of White-fronted Geese flying east—probably returning from a reconnaissance flight to the west after following the Haul Road north. We also saw a Glaucous Gull and a few Arctic ground squirrels, an indication that spring weather was being enjoyed. From there we headed pretty much in a straight line to Milne Point on the edge of the Arctic Ocean where the derelict buildings we wanted to see where located. We had to cross four gravel roads and go under a pipeline three times—some of the Kuparuk Oil Field separated us from our destination.

Once we got to Milne Point, we stopped to look at the old, abandoned NARL buildings plus an old native structure nearby with some sod remaining along the west wall. The roof was partially collapsed and snow filled the inside. Foxes had been all over inside. Isaac found a Snow Bunting nest up in the roof. I wondered if this building is one that Jim's father, Bud, had actually visited or stayed in during his years of travel along the Arctic coast in the 1940s.

Scanning from the top of one of the NARL buildings, Isaac found the small herd of muskoxen out on Pingok Island that we were looking for. We had heard that they had been seen on Pingok. After eating a little snack, Isaac and I headed straight out to Pingok Island from Milne Point. It was even rougher than driving overland, probably because we were angling almost directly across the large snowdrifts. It took about ten minutes to cross the frozen snow-covered ocean ice to arrive at a wide part of this long barrier island where we able to get within about five hundred yards of the muskoxen herd as they fed on a mound on the northern side of the island. There may have been a white fox den on a mound nearby since we watched a white fox attempt to get up on the mound several times only to be charged by one of the muskoxen each time. The fox finally left.

We watched the herd for quite a while before driving on past them to continue on west, down the island. We drove along the northern beach looking for any treasures that might have washed up on the beach. Our beachcombing produced only a few small bones and pieces of bark since there was too much snow cover to easily see anything. We passed a few ptarmigans and earlier saw a lone caribou wandering along the southern shore of the island. Stops were made for a few photos of big ocean ice chunks.

It was getting late by then, so we cut back across the ocean ice to Oliktok Point, where we intersected an ice-road on the river where it was smooth sailing the rest of the way home . . . although Isaac would have been home in about ten minutes if it weren't for his slow-driving mother. I was afraid of skidding on the slick ice of the ice-road, so still didn't go much faster than about thirty mph. (80-90 mph is normal on the freeway-like ice road for the guys) We got home to a late dinner, but had a fun day.

Spring

Harsh winters slowly transition into glorious spring, which is usually considered April into early June. It's different for many Arctic dwellers. For us, there are three main harbingers of spring: more daylight, returning birds, and break-up.

First, it is the rapid increase in sunshine, since the sun comes back quickly after its return in mid-January and its arc above the horizon climbs higher in the sky and it stays up longer each day. Even though the sun gives little or no heat in February and March, it still makes us feel like winter is receding.

This sunshine bouncing off a world of white snow and ice is rejuvenating and intense. It is a time when sunglasses are mandatory, even inside the house at times. Yet this light brings such energy boosts and enjoyment that we think of it as the first steps toward spring. Of course, the sun also works its magic by gradually bringing warmer temperatures and melting snow and ice. By April, the sun is producing considerable warmth and most of our heat in the house is already being generated by radiant heat through the windows. Firewood consumption drops considerably. My many house plants are soaking up the sun and bursting into new growth by then.

The second major spring event for us is the returning birds. We see a few ravens and occasionally a Snowy Owl throughout the winter, but the first migrating birds, which left the Arctic prairie the previous fall, begin showing up in early April. The Snow Bunting, a black and white sparrow-sized bird wins the early-bird award. The males arrive before the females and prepare to entice the females when they arrive to the best nesting spots. Soon various geese and other birds begin arriving to start their reproductive cycle. Pacific Brant nest on our land and around on the entire area of the eastern delta in the thousands; they make up the largest nesting colony of Brant, a sea goose, on the North Slope. There are many

*Black and white
Snow Buntings.*

Spring birds, Lapland Longspur and Snow Buntings, arriving in May. Buildings in back are two-story guest house and a hanger.

other species of waterfowl, like White-fronted Geese, Snow Geese, Tundra Swans, and many species of ducks. Gulls, shorebirds, loons, terns, owls, passerines, and even predator birds fill the land and air around us. Having the thousands of birds back in our world is always a joy and has made for many hours of observing and study of birds for our whole family. Jim and several of our boys are renowned bird experts. Sharing this knowledge and the vast birdlife that fills our summers became one of the highlights of our summer work, both with birding tours and Jim's extensive aerial survey work.

The third and final event considered part of our spring is what is called break-up. The returning sun, the arrival of birds, and spring break-up are pretty much set in stone as far as known yearly events. However, the exact timing can be fickle, differing from year to year by actual date, varying circumstances, and intensity. Some years, it happens with little fanfare, and other years, it roars by with spectacular consequences.

First, let me briefly explain the mechanics of what break-up means. The river has been frozen all winter and by early May, the ice is usually about five to six feet thick in the deeper channels. In the shallow areas of the river, the ice has long since frozen down completely to the bottom of the river and is referred to as grounded ice. Water continues to flow under the ice in the deep channels. As spring melting begins, mostly upstream of the delta area, this water flow under the ice increases. At a point, usually mid-May, the water pressure builds up and forces water up through cracks in the ice and starts flowing on top of the grounded ice. The deep channel ice stays visible as it floats atop the water that is rushing along below it heading out to sea. The entire river, many separate channels by the time it reaches the delta, is still ice-bound, but looking down from an aircraft above, you see lots of water with only ribbons of ice remaining. These ribbons are where the depth of that part of a channel is deep enough for water to continue to flow beneath the ice. Where you see water flowing, it is deceptive, because all the grounded ice is still in place under the water. It is not truly open water yet.

Gradually, over a number of days up to two weeks or so, this grounded ice is eroded, and begins to pop up and float down-river. The thick floating ice is also eroded from the water flowing beneath and the melting occurring from above and can start breaking up and be carried down-river on the turbulent current. During this time, water levels continue to rise, often overflowing the riverbanks and flooding the low-lying areas of land. Some ice chunks become grounded and melt in place but most of the ice chunks are forced down-river and out to sea where they eventually melt. Water levels gradually subside until the river channels reach normal summer conditions. Finally, the river becomes true open water.

Jim secures the boats along the river as flood waters rise, even entering some of our buildings.

Ice breaks up and moves downriver late May or Early June.

However, break-up is fraught with unknowns. No year is the same. Weather plays the main role in how fast or slow the melting takes place, thus affecting water run-off, ice conditions and flooding. In some years, the ice is thicker or jams up along the way, causing colossal consequences. For these reasons, break-up can be a big ordeal for us living on a low island near the face of the Colville River Delta. Almost every year we deal with some flooding of our land. Some years the ice breaks up and moves out to sea easily, entering Harrison Bay in our area with little drama or consequences for us. Other years, we end up with huge ice chunks grounded up on our land along the riverbank, as high water forces ice up and out of normal channels onto flooded areas of land. As water levels recede, this ice is stranded up on land late into June before it's totally melted.

Flooding of our runway and sometimes low-lying buildings is common. This flooding, with or without ice chunks mixed in, causes such a mess. Mud, mud, mud! The break-up water is always laden with silt that gets deposited everywhere the flood waters reach. It takes a lot of rainfall to wash and flush this mud away. We usually have to shovel and sweep it off our walkways between buildings. Some years during the worst flooding, we might have over a foot of water inside some of our buildings. Thankfully our house is raised up three feet on blocking so it is safe from water damage inside. Years with bad flooding always cause many hours of clean-up work outside and inside flooded buildings.

Our most dramatic break-up on record occurred May 22, 2015. An unprecedented event forced four to five-foot-thick ice up on our land bordering the river. It is referred to as ice ride-up and the tremendous water pressure and the sudden breaking of a big ice-jam upriver of our island pushed a mile long section of the deep channel ice, about four to five feet thick, sideways across the river from the far side right up onto our island. Flood waters were still several feet deep over all the shoreline, so this aided the ice to ride-up onto the land.

Since these flood waters had already peaked and started down, we had retired for the night, thinking the worst was over. I was suddenly awakened by our frantically barking dogs as they heard the horrible crushing and grinding sound right outside our back door. When I ran to see what all the commotion was about, I looked out the window and could hardly believe my eyes. What was left of our garage and adjoining generator house were sitting about ten feet closer to the house, twisted and crumpled, like a ramming ball had worked them over soundly. Nothing but closely jammed ice chunks bigger than bumper to bumper semi-trucks were alongside the demolished buildings.

Other floating ice chunks were tightly jammed together bank to bank across the two-thirds-mile-wide river channel. The unusually tumultuous water pressure had broken the upriver ice-jam and pushed so much ice down against the deep-water ice still holding firm across the river from our side, that ice was rammed sideways across the width of the river and pushed right up on land and into the back of our buildings, pushing everything forward over ten feet and mangling both buildings as if they were made of cardboard. A big metal communications tower was crumpled like a toothpick.

Amazingly, our one generator was still running even though the building in which it was housed was crumpled all around it. Getting it shut down before a fire started was paramount. But the building was so crushed, Jim couldn't readily get inside. Finally, he was able to get a ladder and climb down

Jim views the ride-up ice chunks after the flood and destruction of 2015 breakup.

through a hole in the porch roof of the powerhouse. The running generator was nearly knocked off its support blocks and hanging on its side inches off the floor, held only by the exhaust pipe. Jim quickly shut it off, and all was quiet as we stood in shock, surveying the damage.

This was the first time we had ever had a building damaged by ice ride-up, although we had ice ride-up along the edges of our property before. This unusual break-up can be blamed on an early and rapid warming cycle that resulted in rapid melting and much more powerful water dynamics than usual.

The stranded chunks of ice across our riverbank property were still melting into mid-June as we continued weeks of clean-up and repairs. Two of our sons helped us rebuild a new single building to replace the two previous structures. A new shop area was constructed and generators installed.

In contrast to this dynamic break-up in 2015, the 2016 break-up scenario was slow and uneventful with only slight flooding across our property. Every year we hold our breath, waiting to see what break-up has in store for us. Our only recourse is to be prepared with as many items moved above flood levels as possible and hope for the best.

One spring I had an unplanned long ride by snowmachine to get last minute supplies before breakup. This is the story of that ride written soon after it.

A Long Ride

The river flooded, over the grounded ice, eight days ago after a week's unseasonable warm days above freezing. This flooding was eleven days earlier than ever before in our recorded history and several weeks before the usual flooding dates.

Jim and I were caught with some summer supplies still not home. Although they could be gotten later with multiple plane trips, it is much easier to haul them by snowmachine and sled. So, Jim cruised upriver several miles until he could find a good location where he could still cross the river. This was last week, so once across the river he could drive overland to a rendezvous point with a friend who had trucked the supplies from Deadhorse for us. Jim retrieved the freight successfully. It turned cold again, and the flood waters remained stable, so several days later, Jim made another trip over to the mainland to get us some fresh meat—several caribou. Then he made a third trip to collect fresh willow bushes for our yard.

This is where I come in. More mail-order groceries had arrived at the Deadhorse Post Office, plus we still needed some drums of aviation fuel. So, Jim decided it was still safe for another trip across the river and I wanted to go this time. I needed to get over to the road system where we park our pickup truck on a drill pad, five miles east of our house. Of course, the overflow water blocked the straight route we usually travel, so I needed to follow the roundabout route Jim had been using to at least get across the river, and then I could travel overland to where the truck was. I figured I would be able to follow Jim's old trail from last week to get close to where I needed to be.

Jim showed me the route across the river on the map—I only needed to follow his trail. I left at 9 a.m. No problem. It was snowing and very whiteout with limited visibility, but as long as I kept my eyes on the snowmachine trail in front of me, I was fine.

At one point, the trail wound around a lot as Jim had been trying to find a safe way across a creek on which there was quite a bit of overflow water. As I drove along, I pictured being upriver on the creek we have to cross on the way to the pad where the truck sits.

About one and a half hours later I realized something was definitely wrong. Visibility was still poor, but I was seeing bluffs and mounds that were not supposed to be there, plus I should have been at the pad by then, despite the roundabout route. I knew Jim would be worried that I hadn't called him to report being safely at the truck. I stopped to call him on my cell phone and let him know where I was—or maybe he could tell me where I might be. By then I'd figured out that I'd obviously been following the wrong trail, probably the one that took Jim south to hunt caribou, or to get willows.

At that point, I went to pull out my phone. NO PHONE! I had accidentally left my phone sitting on the counter still connected to the charger, and when I had checked my pocket before leaving home to make sure I had the phone, I had actually felt my little camera mistakenly. Now I knew Jim would be worried!

There was a big mound off to my left, so I left Jim's trail and drove over to the high ground to get my bearings. Unfortunately, it was still too poor of visibility to see anything recognizable, but I was quite sure I was on Kachemach Mound—OH MY! So far off-track! There was a slight southwest wind blowing which helped me orient myself, and I drove down off the mound and headed what I thought was east. It turned out to be more south than east. I should have turned straight back the track I had been driving.

However, I kept stopping and re-correcting and had just spotted the top of a derrick which I thought was the oil rig six miles north of our house. It was only a small point on the horizon. I headed for that, figuring I could be sure of my direction once I got closer to it and confirmed it was in fact the oil rig. I should be able to see our home by then too. I had also decided that I would just return home, relieve Jim's worry, get my cell phone, get clearer directions to correct my mistake of taking the wrong trail, and then start out again.

About then Jim came zipping by me and stopped. He had left the house when it became obvious I was long overdue and followed my winding track until he caught up with me. As he drove along, he would say to himself, Why is she following my old trail that goes south? Then as the trail started to cross the Miluveach River, he thought, surely she'll realize where she is now! Oh no, she crossed and is still going. Is she going to go clear to the Kachemach River now?! Jim couldn't leave my trail because visibility was too poor in the whiteout conditions to be able to just look around and find me. He had continued following my trail at a breakneck speed to catch up with me.

When Jim told me it was 11:30 a.m., I was astonished that so much time had passed since I left home. With few words between us, Jim took off in the lead and I realized he was leading me to the truck. It took us forty-five minutes to get there with Jim leading in a straight line. If I had tried to get there on my own once I was sure of my location, it would have probably taken me several more hours. However, I assured Jim I had already decided to return home, had I still been out there on my own.

It was 12:30 p.m. before I was on my way to Deadhorse in the truck and Jim was on his way back home. I knew it would be a long day. By the time I finished the various errands in Deadhorse and got back to the pad on which I parked, it was 6 p.m. Jim was there again to meet me, since we needed two sleds to get the groceries, mail, and fuel drums home. Again, it was a long, roundabout way home via the upriver crossing we had to make to get around the water. It was 9 p.m. by the time we were back in the house, exhausted and hungry.

So, how did I get so turned around out there in the morning? There were several factors. To start out, I had misunderstood Jim about which way to go once I was on the mainland, and how to differentiate the two trails he had made. Secondly, once I was on the wrong trail, even though I was aware that it headed south at first, I thought it would eventually turn and get me to the right spot because I thought I was on the first trail he made to go get supplies at the pad where I needed to be. My focus was solely on the vague trail in front of me. Thirdly, when I crossed the Miluveach River, I thought it was just a bit upriver on the creek we normally have to cross when driving to the pad. Jim had mentioned that he crossed our old trail to the pad at the creek the day he got supplies last week, and this is the trail I thought I was on.

Anyway, I suppose an important lesson learned here is that I should have had my GPS with me even when I thought I would simply be following a trail and not need it. This was a good example of how easily one can get confused on directions when visibility is nil, and few clear landmarks exist.

This is the second time Jim has had to come find me in the last few years when I was lost in a snowstorm and whiteout.

Both times, I was in no danger of severe cold, and would have eventually found my way home (I think), but having Jim find me got me to my destination possibly hours sooner than I would have on my own. Both Jim and I drove many unnecessary miles yesterday due to my mistakes. Jim takes such good care of me—if he can live through the trauma I cause him.

Teena's letter to family, May 13, 2009

Teena hauling supplies by snowmachine.

Summer

Summers are glorious in the Arctic. They are favored for the warm days, bird families all around, green grass, prolific flowers, and fun boat rides. Once the ice is gone from the river and open water prevails, the boats are prepped for use and boating adventures begin. As with my truck travels, I was usually the boat operator after Jim got me all trained up. He was usually too busy flying to have time to play or work with boating ventures. Our family used our small boats both for fun outings for ourselves but also for work, since we had clients to take out on the river as part of their Arctic Adventure Package . . . sometimes to fish, but more often just for sightseeing and birding. That work fell mostly to me, and the boys as they got older.

As the tundra thaws, plant life explodes in the twenty-four-hour sunshine. Grasses, sedges and bushes grow prolifically. Because the topsoil only thaws a few inches, most plants and flowers do not grow tall, but spread out. Flowers have always been a special delight, and I have spent many hours studying and photographing the species covering the Arctic tundra.

The thousands of birds that began arriving in April to start their reproductive cycles of breeding and nesting are hatching and rearing their young. Ducklings, goslings, cygnets,

Capitate Valerian blooms around our land in profusion.

and chicks of so many bird species are everywhere. The air is filled with a concert of bird songs.

New life is everywhere: caribou and muskox calves are frolicking, fox and wolf pups are born and come out of their dens to play, Arctic ground squirrels are soon dashing in and out of their holes, bugs, bees, and other insects abound. Renewal must take place quickly. The accelerated growth of babies across the board is necessary due to the short, warm season. So why is the Arctic such an important area for all this new life? It's the food and vastness.

Plant growth is prolific. There are two critical components that accelerate plant growth in the Arctic: daylight and surface

Herd of several hundred caribou moving across our land as they move through the delta.

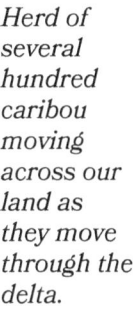

Jim enjoying a calm day on our lake.

water. With many weeks of twenty-four-hour daylight, plants grow at amazing rates. Permafrost across much of the Arctic causes excessive water to remain on the surface of the land, forming thousands of lakes, streams, and bogs. Permafrost is ground that stays permanently frozen year-round. Made up of soil and rocks as well as frozen water, permafrost forms when the depth of winter freezing exceeds the depth of summer thawing, thus creating ground that never has a chance to thaw even during the warm summer months. Some ground-thawing down to about eight to ten inches can occur during summer, allowing the low-lying plant life that does grow.

Teena and boys on a hot day upriver on the Colville in a photo taken by Isaac.

Teena ready to take grandkids on an outing on a cool summer day 2012.

However, the lower layers of frozen ground allow little water to be absorbed. Although the Arctic prairies are virtually deserts by precipitation rates, the rain and snow that does fall has nowhere to go. All this wet land is beneficial for plant growth.

There are over two hundred different species of grasses, shrubs, sedges, and forbs (non-woody flowering plants) found in the Arctic regions. The mosses and lichens also add to the interesting plant life and the dozens of intriguing flower species all provide wildlife food, besides delighting even the most casual of botanists.

Vast hordes of bugs like mosquitoes, crustaceans, and swarms of other marine-source life supply great quantities of food for all the birds and animal life. All the amazing vastness of open, wild Arctic land is a treasure trove of habitat for flora and fauna. It is truly a unique ecosystem bursting with new life every summer.

Temperatures can range from the low thirties to the eighties Fahrenheit, even bringing snow occasionally, but usually average in the forties and fifties. Winds still blow, making dangerous waves on the lakes, river channels, and ocean. Rain falls, mosquitoes buzz, but all in all, it is a wonderful time of year—a time when all growth is accelerated.

Both Jim and I have spent many hours engrossed in finding, studying, and photographing the prolific and fast-growing plants that grace the summer tundra, or prairie, as we often call it. We have dried plant and flower collections and even

Vast numbers of summer birds include the elegant Sabine's Gull and delightful Brant with their darling fluffy gray goslings.

albums full of three-dimensional photocopies of live plants. Our family's wealth of Arctic knowledge and experience includes both flora and fauna. We live a life surrounded by so many natural wonders that it has produced a family of naturalists bent on constantly expanding that environmental base.

This fascination with the natural world is the main reason we developed our extensive museum. It is a testament to what the family treasures about the remote land in which we live: wilderness, wildlife, natural geological and atmospheric beauty, historical artifacts, records and displays of many of the Arctic's natural phenomenon.

Itkillik River Canoe Trip

One of my favorite summer activities is getting out on the river in our boats. 1985 was a very busy summer with a lot of guests to take care of along with four boys and all the family and barnyard duties. Amazingly, we were able to squeeze in one very special adventure. Aaron was three, Isaac was six, Jay was nine, and Derek was thirteen. Harald and Regina Weisker, friends from Germany, arrived to make a canoe trip down the Itkillik River to its confluence with the Colville River and then continue down-river to our home in the delta.

They had arranged to use one of the Helmericks' canoes and have Jim fly them and all their gear up to the chosen beginning spot, about seventy miles inland at a location we called Stinking Hills. This name was derived from the fact that prehistoric animals often melted out of the tall eroding riverbanks of the Itkillik River at this place and even emitted rotten meat smells, since they were not petrified, but had only been frozen for thousands of years. These animal parts were mostly bones, but some flesh was still attached. Here on this North Slope river, as rivers continued the age-old process of cutting into the land bordering the fast-moving water, the banks consisted of mostly permanent frozen ground called permafrost, and the erosion exposed these ancient animal remains to summer thaw.

The Weiskers were preparing for the trip when Regina said to me, "There's another canoe here, why don't you and the boys come with us?" At first, I dismissed the idea, thinking I just couldn't get away from all my duties and responsibilities. But the more I considered it, the more the idea took shape. I had a young gal, Mindy, helping me for the summer. She had learned the ropes well, was competent, and could take care of things, since we had no guests scheduled for the next few weeks. I started getting excited that this spontaneous, incredible adventure might actually happen. Jim gave his approval and went ahead to elicit extra help from his brother, Jeff, with his plane to haul the extra gear and people to the drop-off point.

We had less than twenty-four hours to prepare gear and food for five more people. Camp gear had to be pared down to bare bones. We now had two canoes, gear, and seven people to transport. Jim made two trips with a Piper Super Cub on floats, and Jeff also made two trips with his Cessna 170 on floats, into a lake bordering the winding Itkillik River, to position us for the beginning of our canoe adventure.

It was late evening before we were all settled in our small camp, the planes gone, our first campfire dinner eaten, and the excitement of the full day slowly dissipating as we crawled into our snug sleeping bags.

The next morning broke sunny and warm (as did all the days of our ten-day trip, which was almost unbelievable weather that would leave us with sunburned faces and hands by the end of our trip). Our first day was devoted to exploring around the Stinking Hills area, looking for ancient bones and other treasures that were melting out of the bluffs. It was tiring

Paddling down the Itkillik River with Teena in back, Aaron asleep on the pile of gear, Jay adding his strokes in middle, and Derek in front.
Photo by Weiskers.

hiking, but the few treasures we found, and the beauty of the area was well worth it. I managed to drop my camera in the water when bending over to examine an object, so had to rely on the Weiskers picture taking for the rest of the trip.

Our first day on the river started with a breakfast of coffee, cocoa, and oatmeal, then breaking camp and portaging the loaded canoes down the small stream out of the lake to get into the river. We had no motors; we paddled. My canoe usually had Derek as lead paddler and either Jay or Isaac helping paddle from the middle, and me in the back. Whoever wasn't helping Derek and me paddle would ride with Weiskers in their canoe. Aaron remained with me. We all wore life preservers, and one safety precaution I used for three-year-old Aaron was that his flotation vest was always tied to mine with a strap, so if we ever capsized, he would always be connected to me. Fortunately, we never had to test this plan.

Teena and boys around campfire waiting for dinner. Photo by Weiskers.

Harald and Regina always led the two-canoe party. It was their trip; we were just tag-alongs, so I made sure they got the first opportunity to spot any wildlife coming into view as we paddled along. The river was swift most of the time and twisted and turned like a drunk snake. Around almost every bend, we could come upon moose, caribou, wolves, wolverine, small game like Arctic ground squirrels, raptors like eagles and hawks, or ducks, geese, and other birds. Sometimes it took stopping and climbing up the bank to look out over the

Derek catches dinner before we can eat. Photo by Weiskers.

landscape to see the wildlife, but there were many sandbars and bank-tops with wildlife in plain view.

Our days followed a pattern of breakfast, breaking camp, paddling down-river until early afternoon for a lunch stop, paddling on again until evening when we stopped at a new camp spot, setting up camp, building our evening fire to cook dinner, satisfying ravenous appetites, and then falling exhausted into sleeping bags. However, they were satisfying days full of adventure and wonder. We had something new and exciting around every corner.

Due to limited space and reduced rations, our food supply had to be greatly supplemented with subsistence hunting and gathering. Derek added to the larder with his 22 rifle, bringing in birds to eat such as plovers and ptarmigan; we all fished, and we even harvested flightless geese, when we could catch them. Despite this, the boys were often hungry, especially since they were accustomed to readily available snack foods, which we did not have along on this trip. They had to wait patiently for dinner to cook in the evenings. We usually did not

Teena and boys with mammoth tusk they found in the river in 1985. Photo by Weiskers.

build a cooking fire at the mid-day meal but ate a cold meal. Breakfast was usually a soup made the night before after dinner, reheated in the morning.

Our most exciting day was the third day when we found a most amazing treasure. Our canoe just happened to be leading that day when Derek suddenly called out, "A Tusk!" I looked down where he had been looking just in time to see the shadow of a huge curling object under water disappear as the canoe was swiftly being carried along down-river on the rapid current. Not far behind us was Regina and Harald's canoe.

Harald had heard Derek's cry and thought he had said, "A duck!" Since we were actively trying to obtain food for our next meal, Harald raised the paddle to strike. But then he saw the tusk lying in about two feet of water and he immediately bailed out of the canoe on top of the spot, afraid the current would wash the canoe on past and we'd lose the exact place. Lighting and shadows were constantly making underwater views very difficult, and Derek had been lucky to catch the light just right.

It took a few minutes to get both canoes pulled over to the bank and stopped. We all jumped out and ran back. Sure enough, Harald was struggling to lift a huge mammoth tusk out of the water. What a find! Harald was dripping wet but had a big smile on his face. We took many pictures and discussed what a great addition to the Helmericks Colville Museum the tusk would make. Strapping the tusk crosswise over Weisker's canoe, we continued on down-river. The great weight of the tusk was a big drag on our forward momentum. What to do?

That problem was solved the next day when Jim flew over us with the Cessna 206 on floats. Jim had been busy off completing other flying jobs and had decided to check on us as he flew back home. He flew the river looking for us and when he spotted us, he circled to let us know he was there. He found a big lake near the river up ahead of us in which to land. We paddled on, keeping a close watch on where we hoped Jim had landed.

It wasn't long before we saw Jim waiting on the bank for us to arrive. He had walked over from the lake to the river to meet us. There were lots of excited stories to exchange and plans to make. Jim and Harald carried the tusk back to the floatplane and Jim sent all the food he could rustle up from his own survival gear to give us for our continuing trip. He even gave me the clean shirt off his back, so I could replace the only shirt I had brought with me which was getting quite soiled by then.

It was a relief to have the weight of the tusk gone, plus extra supplies added to our rations as we continued down the Itkillik River. Days were filled with beautiful scenery, glorious sunshine, and wildlife viewing. Arctic Char and grayling, and succulent young geese were consumed at each night's camp.

When we reached the confluence of the Itkillik and Colville River, about thirty miles upriver from our homesite, we encountered very strong northeast headwinds. We were already behind schedule to return, so we tried paddling against the wind, but finally had to retreat back behind the tall banks of the Itkillik River to set up camp and wait. We had no phones or radios in those days.

The next morning, the wind seemed down a bit, so we packed up the canoes and started down river again. We were able to make slow headway, but it was miserably cold in the wind and high waves. We hugged the riverbank to avoid the worst of the waves and had to stop periodically to climb up on the bank and run around to warm up.

After several hours of this, we looked up to see a big white boat coming toward us. I soon recognized it as our workboat with Jim at the helm. He had come to rescue us, knowing how miserable canoeing would be in the high wind and waves, and that we were already overdue. We all cheered. We were a cold, bedraggled crew happy to be relieved of any further paddling against the angry wind.

Jim had to figure out how to accommodate us, all our gear, and two canoes in his one boat. It took a little ingenuity to strap one canoe up on top of the bigger boat and rig a towline for the second canoe behind. Some gear was left in the canoe under tow. Then we all piled in and snuggled down for the long, cold ride home which took several hours.

Fall arriving as ptarmigan start turning white for winter and grass is brown.

Fall sunset over our lake.

Fall

Fall comes gradually as summer wanes. It sneaks up on you, and you suddenly realize that the green grass has turned brown, the flowers have gone to seed, the willow leaves are red, yellow and brown, most migratory birds are gone, and the winds are getting colder. This starts in late August and continues into October, when the land completely freezes up.

Fall is the time to get the best Dall sheep, caribou, and moose meat. Animals are fat from summer grazing and their coats are at a prime for use. Most of our year's meat needs were met with those animals taken during guiding other hunters. As local residents we are allowed to hunt caribou all year, except during May calving season, so we can even take caribou in much of spring, if we need fresh meat.

Fall becomes a waiting game: waiting for colder temperatures, waiting for winter's snow and ice to build up so travel across the frozen terrain can begin, and waiting to start our fishing operation under the ice. Boats are retired and floatplanes need landing gear exchanged for wheels. Summer equipment and tools must be put away and winter gear brought out. Snowmachines are prepped for use as they are the winter workhorses.

One joy of the fall season is gorgeous sunrises and sunsets, even though they are the harbingers of dark days ahead. In our part of the world, the twenty-four-hour sun has been getting lower in the sky since June and starts setting again on July 29. Daylight each day gets less and less, until November 24,

Our Carolina Skiff parked at the camp where we spent two nights.

when it disappears below the horizon for the rest of that year. During these days, the low sun can create amazingly beautiful skies when near the horizon, whether just below or just above.

Camping and Colville River Trip

In the fall of 1998, the kids and I were treated to another fun river trip up the Colville River. Jim had flown the floatplane south of the Itkillik River, a tributary to the Colville, and spent the night on a big lake near the river where he shot three big caribou the next morning. After he got home with all the fresh meat, he suggested we might want to go camping upriver. He had seen fresh bear tracks and Isaac had a bear tag for this fall and hoped to get a grizzly. No bears had been seen here in the delta over the past few weeks. There were plenty more caribou up there too if we wanted to get more meat for winter.

Of course, I jumped at the chance. I'm always ready for an adventure. Isaac decided he'd rather stay on the Colville River though because we weren't sure we could get the boat up to the area where Jim had been. We had been eager to make a trip further upriver on the Colville anyway. So, we got our camping gear ready, got the spare gas jugs filled, and left Saturday morning in the Carolina Skiff, our nineteen foot river boat. The wind was down, and it was partly cloudy—quite pleasant, despite being in the mid-thirties Fahrenheit.

Along the way upriver we made several quick stops for Isaac to scope around. All we saw were a few muskoxen at the upper outlet of the Kachemach River. Pingo Beach and Buffalo

The three hundred-foot-high Colville River Bluffs where geologists believe the bottom layer of the bluffs exposes regions from eighty million years ago. This is where they search for dinosaur bones.

Lookout (Iñupiat name: Poviqsok) was one of our stops, and later Ocean Point where Jay, Isaac, and I had camped once before. The drum still sits on top of the beginning of the high bluffs. It is a prominent stopping place for many river travelers.

The next stop was the upriver side of the big sandbar where Jim and I used to land with the *Golden Plover* to look for shells or mammoth bones and tusks years ago. Now it is the sandbar used by the University of Alaska Fairbanks people digging for dinosaur bones in the bluffs, so we've taken to calling it Dinosaur Bar.

I stopped climbing the bluff at each stop after Ocean Point. One climb was all my legs could manage. The bluffs are usually about one hundred fifty to two hundred feet straight up. They are crumbling dirt, mud, and sod with grasses and willows poking out in places they can grab hold to grow. As with many high river bluffs, there are rows upon rows of vertical ridges between gullies where run-off water has cut deep fissures in the banks.

Climbing means using a gully and working your way back and forth upward, grabbing willow branches to help pull yourself up until you reach the top. The view is worth the climb! The high banks run along the west side of the river and rise up to a flat plateau of tundra. The east side of the river is lowlands with gravel bars, braided side channels, and patches of tall willows or alder bushes. From the top of the high banks, you can see for miles around.

By the time we reached the high bluffs, the water was churning along quite fast and could grab the boat and carry us down-river rapidly when we cut the engine. It is neat to see the swirling, bubbling water after being used to the calm, sluggish water of the delta region. We came upon occasional camping spots, evident by debris left behind by careless campers, but mostly we were traveling through pristine wilderness.

We finally found a suitable spot to camp on the low side of the river that had a small inlet, tall willows (up to fifteen feet or so), and flat spot for the tent. As soon as we unloaded the boat, Isaac built a campfire and got the tea kettle heating. While getting the tent ready to put up and the woodstove out of its bag, I came to the realization that we were missing the stovepipe for the woodstove that goes inside the tent!! I had made the mistake of thinking the pipe was inside the stove like some of our other little stoves. I had my favorite stove, the one which Dad Helmericks had repaired the broken door latch for me several years ago. I dejectedly remembered that the pipe was in another bag we forgot to bring. Oh, my, can I survive without the warmth of a woodstove in the tent? We decided we had no choice, and we weren't going back! The tent went up, the air mattresses blown up, bags unrolled, and other camping conveniences fixed up. Then the boys went off to other things while I enjoyed hot coffee by our campfire.

Isaac caught a big grayling right by camp in the little notch in the river's edge. A small stream ran down into the riling water that swirled into the indentation in the four-foot riverbank, and it was a perfect place for fish to hang out to eat what ran out of the stream that drained a marshy area higher up. Three more fish were soon on the bank; I suggested Isaac hold off catching any more until we ate the ones we had. Aaron went out and soon returned with a ptarmigan to add to the larder.

Dinner was soon cooked. We always carry a fire-grate in the boat that makes cooking over the open fire convenient. I made a rice dish with cut-up boiled caribou tongue in it. Yummy! Fresh tongue from Jim's caribou. We set up the wood stove outside by the open fire so I could use it for a table. We do have a nice folding camp table and folding chairs, but we had left those behind trying to keep our load as light as possible in order to conserve gas to use for more exploring. Of course, Aaron had the marshmallows out for dessert.

We enjoyed a peaceful evening, and we all went walking around to explore the area. There was a small hill several hundred yards behind camp and a lake on the other side. Just down the bank near an alder patch was a small crater that had been a pond but had broken out into the river and drained. It had happened recently because all the pond's underwater plants were still there lying flat and drying out at the bottom of the sunken area. The tall willow bushes were quite thick behind the tent and around where we had the fire. I like being in a sheltered spot like that. We were able to stretch a rope between willow branches up over the fire to hang things to dry.

Large moose tracks with little ones alongside covered the dried muddy area by the stream's edge. Muskoxen tracks also crisscrossed the area. Critter tracks were here and there, including fox tracks. Ptarmigan were all around, Northern Shrikes called in the bushes, redpolls flitted between the willows, and a wagtail was around. All day we had been seeing, and especially hearing, large flocks of White-fronted Geese flying overhead as they migrated south. Glaucous Gulls squawked at us as soon as they found us in their area. There had been a few Rough-legged Hawks still soaring over the bluffs, although all the nests were empty and most of the various hawks and falcons had already gone south.

It was dark by 10 p.m., so we climbed into our sleeping bags about then. I did have our red kerosene lantern hanging from the tent peak to light the inside of the tent as we settled in.

Sunday morning, I was awakened at 5:30 a.m. by geese calling. I could picture the big V shape up high in the sky. After getting up, I realized I wouldn't have seen them at all. A heavy fog lay over us; we could barely see the far side of the river. We were in a silent world, and the ground was hard and white with frost. It had gotten down in the high twenties Fahrenheit during the night, and it was several hours before it warmed up above freezing. Although Isaac slept warmly in his better-quality bag, Aaron and I had gotten cold during the night, mainly our feet. The fog lifted gradually, and the high bluffs slowly appeared out of the mist.

We soon had a roaring fire outside to cook breakfast, and warm ourselves. Isaac had used his single-burner camp stove to heat water quickly so we could have coffee and cocoa first. We ate hot oatmeal and then each had a grayling for our second course. Isaac and Aaron went bird hunting then while I enjoyed the fire and wrote in my journal. When they got back, we decided to button up the camp and go exploring upriver.

We had a fun day, getting as far inland as Sentinel Hill. We watched five muskoxen on the tip of a sandbar—three cows, a yearling bull, and a calf. We made a side trip up a tributary called Kogosukruk River. Its mouth is about six miles down-river from Sentinel Hill. We had to use our backup engine to make our way up the shallow, fast-flowing river, and finally decided to turn back. Before leaving, the boys walked across a pretty valley west of the small river to climb a hill to look around. Our map showed it was 167 feet tall. They saw a small herd of caribou upriver, but too far away to be practical to go after. Black chunks of coal were lying on the sandbar where we had pulled up the boat. We could see the seams of low-grade coal running along the banks that were ten to twenty feet high.

Three other boats crossed our path during the day. I talked to one group of three people from Nuiqsut village who stopped to talk to me (my boys were up on the high bluff) while we were stopped on a sandbar. They were looking for moose to hunt and also fishing for grayling and char. They didn't stay long, and I went back to reading my book until the boys got back.

We returned to our camp about 8:30 p.m. that night. We just had time to cook dinner of ptarmigan and pintail meat and settle in for the night before dark. I had the idea of heating rocks in the campfire to put in a sock and then in our sleeping bags to keep our feet warm. Mind you, I'd never done it before, but I had read about doing it. We weren't sure if the hot rock could scorch the bag or not. They did not and it worked great.

Monday morning came quickly. We'd all slept like logs. No thrashing or lying awake listening for intruder noises like

Our Carolina Skiff was our favorite river-cruising boat.

the night before. Plus, it didn't get as cold during the night. It did freeze but stayed warmer most of the time. We slept a lot warmer and I'm sure the rocks added to the comfort. There was no fog the second morning and blue sky was mixed with a few wispy clouds. It was nearly calm. After breakfast, we broke down the camp and loaded the boat up. We had decided to mosey on down the river and see what the day would bring. We continued to stop at various places to climb the high bluffs and look around. While we were on the top of the bluff at Dinosaur Sandbar, a C-180 came in to land below us. We left while it was still there, so we didn't know if a hunter was being dropped off or what the plane was doing there.

About a mile upriver from Ocean Point, Aaron tried for a caribou in a group of four bulls back inland a little way from the top of the bluff. Aaron missed his first shot and decided not to try again as the caribou were walking away from the river, showing only their butts and making the packing of meat more difficult if one were shot. No bears or moose were seen.

We stopped at Jimmy Creek just up from Pingo Beach and took the boat as far up that little creek as we could go. It is a pretty area hidden between ten-foot banks lined with willow and alder bushes.

From there we bundled up tightly, planning to keep going until we got home. It gets so cold in the boat even when it's calm, since we create our own wind of twenty to thirty mph with the forward speed of the boat. Fortunately, it did remain calm or with very little wind on the run back down the river.

We stopped to watch a lone bull muskox at the mouth of the Kachemach River. It was unafraid of us and let us climb the bank to watch him from about twenty feet away. Isaac thought it was probably the same bull that he and Derek watched on an earlier occasion, also unperturbed at them being so close. There were over one hundred swans around the mouth of the Kachemach, and more around Round Island, as we called it, and the mouth of the Miluveach River. We also saw a number of river seals here and there along the river.

We got home at about 6:30 that evening. Jim wasn't expecting us until Tuesday, but he was glad for us to be home. Toby, our dog, is always an explosion of enthusiasm to see anyone of us who have been gone for a while. I was glad to warm my feet by the stove. You'd think I'd have a system down pat by now for staying warm in the boat, but I didn't have the right footgear for fall-time travel in the boat. Dumb!

To end this saga, I must add that ironically while Isaac was upriver looking for a bear, there were two bears down near our island. Jim had planned to fly to Deadhorse for mail while we were gone, but he didn't dare leave for fear one of the bears would get on the island and cause trouble. Isaac went on to get his bear later Monday night, but that is another story.

Chapter 9
Weather Rules

Effects of Weather

Our lives are ruled by what the weather is doing. Although the weather has minimal effects to daily life inside our comfortable home, it continually affects transportation of people and supplies, or any travel plans away from home. No matter what activities are planned, we always have to be prepared to face delays or plan changes because of bad weather. Patience in the face of such delays must be endured or we would have gone crazy or left the Arctic long ago.

In summer, low or nonexistent visibility due to fog or high winds restrict both flying and boating which are the only means of leaving our island home that time of year. If you can't see where you are going, you can't fly, plus high winds can also keep smaller planes grounded. Before GPS guidance systems, fog restricted most boating also, since the boating channel to reach a road system is narrow and tricky to negotiate in places. These high winds also create dangerous waves in the river or bay. We all followed strict safety-first protocol, so many a day started with hopeful plans that disintegrated throughout the day as fog or high winds persisted.

In winter, extreme cold is a major detriment to winter travels, since we normally restrict motorized travel below -30 F Some years during these cold, dark days of winter, we put our airplanes away in our hanger and do not maintain our runway which is not lighted and soon covered with large snowdrifts. Obviously, the boats are no longer of use in winter.

Thus, we become dependent upon ground transportation by all-terrain vehicles (ATVs) across the frozen landscape for any travel to and from home. Although this ground travel across our winter landscape can be a wide-open window of travel, the restrictions caused by storms or whiteout conditions happen with predicted regularity. High winds causing blowing snow can bring visibility down to zero-zero. Even on the few roads in the North Slope villages or within the oil field, poor visibility can stop all travel.

Weather delays are unfortunately common. One delay that was particularly hard on me was a delay in the early 2000s that kept me from attending my niece's wedding in Homer, located at the opposite end of Alaska from my home. This delay was definitely bad weather—days and days of fog along Alaska's North Slope. I was home on the Colville River and Jim needed to get me to Deadhorse in Prudhoe Bay, sixty miles east of us, by small plane, so I could catch the commercial jet to Anchorage. Extreme low visibility due to persistent fog lasted for several days.

Jim could not fly. I tried to be patient, but I was broken-hearted when the wedding day came and went as I sat in the fog on the Colville. When the fog finally lifted, I decided to go anyway just to visit the many friends and family gathered for the event, so Jim flew me to Deadhorse. I had remained stoic over the weather delays. It was out of my hands, and I just had to endure. However, I finally succumbed to tears while relating my weather-delay saga to a friend in Deadhorse while waiting for the jet to whisk me on south. She consoled me, and I felt a bit hypocritical, since I was usually the one preaching the virtue of patience in the face of weather delays.

I was thwarted again in Anchorage from continuing on by fog grounding the planes in Homer. I waited at the Anchorage terminal, but finally gave up trying to even make an appearance at the after-wedding functions being held in Homer. I never made it. Fortunately, I was only a delinquent wedding guest, and not a critical member of the wedding party, and later I got to see many family members and friends in Anchorage.

Big Storm—Slope-wide

Most people know life isn't all peaches and cream. I would be remiss to exclude all references to negative experiences. My family has endured our share of tough times and many adversities are too personal and tender-hearted to share in this book, but to be true to life, I must share a few traumatic and white-knuckle episodes. I have already described a few medical emergencies and weather-related challenges we faced, but have yet to tell the story of the biggest storm we've ever had to endure that produced significant damage to our home and property.

On the night of February 25, 1989, our homesite and the entire North Slope coastal area was pummeled by the worst wind ever recorded in recent times. It was a freak wind, over one hundred mph, which left unexpected and substantial damage in its wake in both coastal villages and oil field facilities.

The three younger boys and I were alone, as Jim and our oldest son, Derek, were both gone. Jim was driving heavy equipment on an oil field job in Prudhoe Bay and Derek was on a school-sponsored field trip in Fairbanks. Weather advisories on the radio alerted communities along the Beaufort Sea coastline of coming northeast winds, nothing unusual for local residents used to frequent windstorms. Pilots of small aircraft secured their planes accordingly, tied facing into the forecasted wind. Here at our homesite, we had everything secured for our usual winds. We were snug in a warm house and our two planes, the Cessna 206 and Piper Super Cub, were securely tied and facing into the northeast. All was under control. I was used to high winds and our mid-winter world of white, snow and freezing temperatures.

We had been living in the downstairs of our new house for less than a year and the entire second story was still unfinished. Although the entire roof and outer walls and most windows of the upstairs were finished, the inner room walls were unfinished and windows for my large sunroom still missing. Plywood simply covered those openings from the inside. This unfinished upper story was isolated from the first story with a stairway's door and insulation. The little oil furnace Jim had hooked up for me before leaving so I wouldn't have to cut firewood for our main stove, was purring along and keeping the main floor warm and cozy despite the slowly increasing northeast wind.

I went to bed early after getting the boys tucked in for the night and fell right to sleep. About midnight, I was suddenly awakened by a loud roaring noise outside and a snapping and clanking noise inside I couldn't identify. I was used to the sounds of high winds swooshing and clattering against the house, but something wasn't right!

I jumped out of bed in alarm. I ran into the living room area to find the unfamiliar clanking noise. Behind the oil-stove heater, I discovered the stovepipe damper was flapping open and closed like I'd never seen before. That scared me. What was happening? I couldn't see anything out the windows in the dark, but I was confused because it sounded like the wind and blowing snow was hitting directly against the southwest side of the house. How could that be?

The forecast was for northeast winds . . . exactly from the opposite direction and certainly not this fierce! But there was no denying it. I was soon convinced that this alarming wind was indeed smashing into us from the SOUTHWEST! The whole house was shaking by then. I quickly got dressed and woke the boys and told them to dress. I didn't know what was happening, but I wanted us prepared for whatever we had to do. We even gathered all our outdoor gear in case we ended up out in the storm.

Several opening windows on the main floor began to bang as hinges bent. Thankfully, they were holding together despite the beating they were getting. I closed the doors to those rooms in case the windows broke in. We heard crashing noises upstairs in the unfinished part of the house, but I was afraid to open up the stairway between the two floors. I became afraid of smoke and fire dangers as the oil-stove damper kept banging ferociously and the chimney pipe shook. What if it all blew apart? I shut the stove off just in case. We had our parkas to put on as the house cooled down.

Then I thought of the airplanes tied down outside, tailed into this unbelievable southwest wind. I knew it would be BAD! I had to wait for some daylight before I could even check. The boys and I huddled together and tried to get a bit more sleep while we waited.

Being mid-winter, it was late morning before there was any daylight. However, blowing snow obscured visibility to only a few feet. There was no way to see the C-206 tied on her parking pad two hundred yards away. Jay, only thirteen, and I had to bundle up and brave the storm to check the planes, even though I knew there probably was not much we could do. It was a struggle to stand upright as we were blown along downwind. As the C-206 came into view, it definitely looked a bit catawampus, yet still sat securely on the pad. Then I realized the tail was taking a beating, as the force of the wind pushed against the vertical stabilizer and had it bent far to the side.

Normally when the plane faced into the wind as it should have been, the stabilizer would be straight in line with the rest of the upright tail. Jay and I could force it back in line against the wind but it would not hold, so I decided to try and brace it. It took an hour or more to gather what we needed so we could rig up some braces to hold it in place to prevent further damage. With wooden survey slats and heavy string, we tied doubled slats across the front of the tail and vertical stabilizers at top, middle, and bottom. That held the stabilizer in place. I also tied a second set of tie-down ropes to the wings for added safety. That was all we could do. With such high winds, even if Jim had been here with us, there would have been no way we could have turned the plane into the wind.

Next, we stumbled along as we let the wind push us down another three hundred yards to where the Piper Super Cub was tied. It was slightly protected from the wind by big drifts of snow made by earlier winds, so I was hopeful. But as the plane materialized out of the blowing snow, my heart sank. There our *Golden Plover* lay in the snow like a crippled bird. The once beautiful flying machine, that was like a member of our family, was lying there with her wings folded forward toward her nose like a broken-winged bird with wings shielding her face. I was broken-hearted. One wing strut had snapped, and the other bent, as both wings lay limp in the snow with the wind beating against them endlessly. I dreaded having to tell Jim that his special Girl, as he called her, was terribly broken.

Jay and I braced the tail as we had done with the bigger plane, but not much else could be done. Heading back to the house facing the wind, we were mostly forced to crawl, since standing was impossible. Once home, we had to strip out of all our wet clothing, since the force of the wind had driven snow through zippers and minute cracks in our jackets. The snow was melting due to body warmth and all our exertion.

I talked to Jim on the phone and through choking tears, told him about the crumpled *Golden Plover*. He took the news stoically and reassured and comforted me with words of thankfulness that the boys and I were safe, and that buildings and planes could be repaired. He said he was trying to get home as soon as he could. However, these plans were thwarted for many days. Everyone thought the storm was abating, only to have the wind increase again even worse into the second day. Winds were reported to be 107 mph in Prudhoe Bay, and possibly higher to the east toward our place. Huge snowdrifts blocked all roads and people were stranded in stalled vehicles all over the oil field roads. Many rescue operations with ATV vehicles (with tracks for off-road) were underway to pick up stranded personnel.

The kids and I had to hunker-down for another day, and I wondered what else was being damaged besides the planes. Windows and even house walls were getting sucked in and out several inches. That was truly frightening! Would the house hold together? Several more windows developed broken latches and were banging alarmingly. Earlier we had secured heavy-duty plastic across the inside of most windows as added insulation against the winter cold, and these plastic barriers were stretched taut with the wind pressure. I nailed wooden slats across these windows for reinforcement.

Jay and I fought our way out to the C-206 another time to check on our tail-bracing job. As we slowly struggled through the blowing snow, I noticed several six-foot-long pieces of plywood strips stuck in the snow on the ground downwind of the house. It dawned on me that they had come off our roof. The force of the wind had ripped them loose which meant the waterproofing material that the slats secured to the roof was getting torn off the roof, too. When we reached the plane, we were disheartened to see all our earlier labor to protect the tail from getting further bent was for naught. The slats we had used had been snapped like toothpicks and a few broken pieces stuck out of the snow here and there. We needed something stronger, and I thought of those bigger plywood strips lying in the snow back toward the house. Jay and I gathered up four of them and again struggled to tie them together across the two upright tail sections. We rolled a partially full fifty-five-gallon drum of fuel over to the back of the plane, so I had something to stand on while Jay held the vertical stabilizer straight again. Thankfully these proved to hold throughout the rest of the storm.

All was still stable with the plane—there was nothing further we could do there, so Jay and I returned to the house. I decided to check on what was happening upstairs. What a shock awaited our eyes! SNOW blanketed everything! The crash that we had heard earlier was the big pieces of plywood being torn loose and banging down off the sunroom window

Teena and Jay brace the damaged airplane tail with stronger slats.

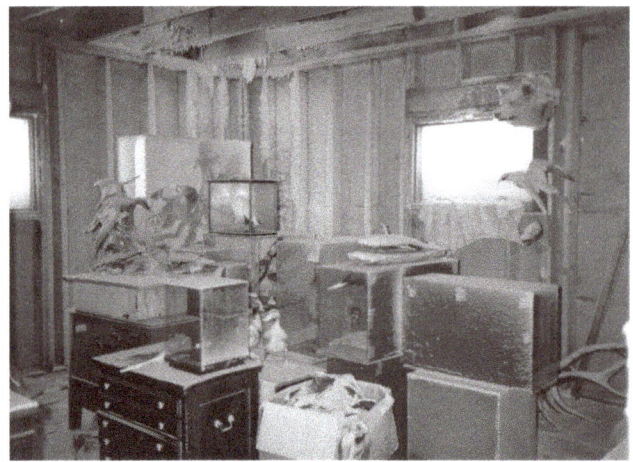

The big storm of 1989 left unfinished rooms in the upstairs of the lodge covered in snow. These rooms were full of museum cases and many other items that needed hours of cleaning.

openings. Now there were two huge gaping holes in the outer wall with wind-driven snow cascading throughout the entire upstairs, including all the museum display cases, animal wall mounts, furniture, everything!

We had no idea how long this storm would last, so Jay and I strained to nail the pieces of plywood back in place and braced them with large two by six planks of wood. It took a lot of maneuvering to push the plywood back against the blizzard-strength wind. That was all we could do for the time being. We returned downstairs to wait out the storm with the two younger boys. We stayed together and kept our heavy winter outdoor gear handy. I was glad I had turned off our oil-burning stove for fear that the rattling chimney would blow apart and didn't want to deal with the possibility of smoke filling the house. It was another very restless night.

Monday morning, February 27, arrived clear, cold, and CALM! It was time to assess the damage. I had heard on the radio broadcast from Barrow that wind damage was being reported across the North Slope coastal area. Small planes suffered severe damage in both Barrow and Deadhorse parking areas. Windows and roofs were destroyed. I talked to Jim on the phone again and reported on our situation, letting him know we were safe and the stove was back on and again warming the house. The chimney for our oil stove had been rattled apart where it passes through the attic, but it hadn't pulled out of the roof opening. I had gotten it reattached before I had restarted the stove.

The boys and I decided to go outside and briefly assess the damage around our place. We needed to care for the animals. Most of our house roof was stripped bare of the waterproofing cover. Broken slats and pieces of torn waterproof liner that hadn't completely blown away were sticking out of snowdrifts here and there downwind of the house. We noticed our attic roof-hatch had blown off and part of our attic was full of snow. The big sliding door on the shop had been completely blown off its roller track and several rooms of that building were full of snow. Other buildings had rooms full of snow also. Fortunately, no other buildings had roof damage, since they all had finished roofs.

Next, we checked on the animals. The sled-dogs had come through the storm unscathed. They know how to curl up and let the snow accumulate around their body as a warm shield to protect them from the wind. Only our old dog, Kaiser, had not been able to completely retain his body heat, snow had beat into his fur, and couldn't just be shaken off like the other dogs could do. We brought him into the house for the snow and ice to melt out of his fur. All the dogs were excited to get extra food that day.

We carried extra water to the barn for the goats, chickens, and rabbits. The barn porch door had blown open and filled that area with snow, but fortunately the inner door had held. The animals were fine.

We weren't so fortunate with our small two-story guesthouse, as both porch and inner door faced directly into the worst wind and those doors had blown in, blanketing both stories with about two inches of snow over all. Jay shoveled out the doorways so we could close the doors properly. Since it was still well below freezing, there was no rush with the arduous job of removing all the snow in unused buildings. That would take months.

We checked out equipment and outdoor items and discovered our snowmachine cover was nowhere to be seen. It was probably blown to the North Pole. The windshield was gone. Remember, everything outdoors had been prepped for a northeast wind, and the snowmachine, like the planes, was parked facing into the wind. A heavy wooden sled still hitched to the back of the snowmachine was flipped upside-down and thrown sideways, lying almost parallel to it. Our wheelbarrow, sitting in the lee of the house, had a big dent on its side where a chunk of ten-by-ten timber had been tossed against it from our firewood pile about ten feet away. Our little smokehouse structure, partially buried in a snowdrift from earlier high winds, was missing its roof and most of the front. Surprisingly, the snow-covered racks full of frozen meat were still there. The building supplies stacked around the yard had also been protected from the freak storm by snowdrifts covering them from earlier winds.

In checking the planes again, the stabilizer braces had held the second time, but now we had another problem. The nose of the C-206 was up in the air at an unnatural angle and the tail partially buried in a snowdrift. We dug out the buried horizontal stabilizers and tried to lift the tail back up so the nose wheel was back on the ground. It was too heavy! That job had to wait for Jim. We later discovered that the back half of the fuselage was packed full of snow, causing the excessive weight. It had to melt out.

It took several more days before oil field roads were cleared enough for vehicles to begin moving again and Jim and Derek could make their way home. It took days to clean the snow out of the upstairs and work to muck out the snow from critical spaces in the out-buildings. Some unused spaces had to wait for the spring thaw to melt and dry out. Eventually, Jim was able to get the C-206 tail repaired. He dismantled the *Golden Plover* for shipment to Fairbanks to be rebuilt. We repaired the house roof and finished with well-secured aluminum roofing.

There were other trials and ordeals to face in coming years, such as devastating floods and destructive ice-ride-up incidents, but never another hurricane storm of this intensity. However, we did have another extremely traumatic boat-related episode I look back on in shame for I felt terribly responsible for letting it happen.

Day of Trauma—Wild River

It turned out to be one of the most terrifying days of my life. It was summer 1990 and we were well into the boating season. The high water of break-up had receded long ago, and low water of late summer had forced us to move the two boats down the riverbank from our house about a mile to a spot that had deeper water close to shore, making mooring the boats easier. Otherwise, you had to walk the boat in and out through the shallows to access the boat dock near the house.

Having to keep the boats moored away from easy monitoring distance during bad weather was a pain. It usually meant a walk or six-wheeler ride down to the mooring area to double check anchor lines and boat stability (not getting swamped) when storms blew up.

Storm tides in this part of the north can rise or fall many feet even though normal tide movements are minimal. Depending on the wind direction, big waves or rising water must be watched to see that the boats remain securely anchored and well protected from getting swamped by waves. This was one of those mornings. A southwest wind had picked up into storm proportions, blowing well over thirty to forty mph. I asked Derek, then eighteen, to go down and check the boats. He returned in a panic that our large workboat had broken its anchor rope and had blown across the river to the far side.

We got the binoculars and could just barely see it across the distance of about one and a half miles of crashing waves and fog. We were both scared it would get swamped and sunk. I told Derek and Jay, then fifteen, that they'd better go get it and he could drive the workboat back and Jay could bring the aluminum skiff back across the river. They didn't hesitate, got their outdoor gear on and I drove them down to the skiff in our track-truck. Jim was home but busy in another part of our large lodge and not aware of what was going on.

I stayed by the river-launching area to watch the boys cross the river through the wild waves, making sure they got safely to the other side. Using binoculars, I saw Derek get in the workboat, start the fifty hp outboard engine and then both boys started back across the expanse of tumultuous water. Jay led in the silver skiff with the white workboat following behind.

I drove home and figured that was that—thank goodness, they had successfully retrieved the break-away boat and would soon have all safely secured back on our side of the river.

However, Jay got back to the house a little bit later and no Derek. When I asked why, Jay said something happened, he didn't know what, but Derek did not get back to shore behind him and it looked like he was back in the pounding waves on the far side of the river. We got the binoculars and studied the situation from the windows of the second story of the house. It was hard to make out what was going on, but the boat was near the far riverbank, getting pounded fiercely by the winds and waves and Derek was hanging over the back transom, hands gripping something down near the water. After further study, I decided there was no engine in sight on the transom where it should be and something drastic had happened. What in the world was going on? Jay offered to go back over in the little skiff. Derek obviously needed help, so I let him go.

Once Jay was halfway across the river in the worsening storm, I realized I had been extremely foolish to let either boy leave the safety of land in such a storm! Even with the binoculars, I would lose sight of Jay, the little silver boat only a speck between giant waves, and I was frantic that he was gone. I had put my sons at risk of drowning! I could just hear Jim lecturing us all about safety and how he would say NO equipment is worth chancing serious injury or death. I knew he would be furious if he knew I had let the boys take a boat out in such a storm. WHAT WAS I THINKING?!

I sat in the track-truck down by the river's edge praying for the boys' safety harder than I'd ever prayed before. Finally, after fifteen minutes or so of agonizing despair, I caught sight of the little silver boat pulling up beside the workboat and two heads bent over doing something together.

After a time of bewilderment over what could be going on, I saw one of the boys standing up on top of the far riverbank, and both boats together just below the bank. Shortly after this both boys were headed back across the river in the silver skiff.

They made it! I no longer cared in the least what happened to the workboat or its engine, just that the boys were back alive and safe.

Both boys were soaked to the skin and Derek was exhausted and had bloody hands that needed medical care. The story slowly came out as we drove back to the house.

Derek had gotten in the workboat, got the engine started, and began following Jay back across the river. However, as he gave the engine a burst of speed to lessen the distance between himself and Jay, the large fifty hp engine suddenly flew off the transom into the thrashing water. Derek's heart had lurched when he realized he had forgotten to check the clamps holding the engine tightly to the transom.

Another no-no: only one small safety rope was attached to the engine. Why wasn't a stronger, second rope attached as it should have been? Derek grabbed the flimsy rope, thinking the weight of the engine would surely snap the line. He was afraid to let go and lose the expensive engine down into the depths of the deep channel. As he hung on for dear life, the wind and waves swung the boat around stern into the storm, and waves were pounding him with water and filling the boat. The boat was slowly pushed back toward the far shore.

Finally, the engine touched bottom and acted as an anchor, but Derek kept his hold on the rope despite his hands being rubbed raw and he would give a mighty pull every time a wave lifted the boat and engine so he would be pushed ever closer to shallower water. By that time, Jay had made it back out to help and together they both continued working the boat and dangling engine into shallower water and closer to shore.

Once the boat became grounded, the boys used the little boat to get ashore and anchor the big boat to a large stick driven into the ground. They weren't strong enough to pull the big engine out of the water and had to leave it, but at least its location was known, and it could be retrieved after the storm, along with the boat.

In retrospect, our unsinkable workboat would have been fine had we just left it alone in the first place and waited for the storm's end to retrieve it. It would not have sunk had it swamped, for it was swamped by the time Derek got it to shallows on the far side, and yet it remained afloat—one of the attributes of our workboat was that it is unsinkable. With their dad's help, the boys were able to retrieve the it and the sunken engine a day later after the storm ended. The engine was totally dismantled and repaired to run many more years.

However, I learned a hard lesson about thinking more clearly and carefully before making rash decisions that endangered lives unnecessarily. I thank the Lord that He protected my sons that day, despite my foolish actions.

More Weather Challenges!

A different kind of weather-related incident occurred in the 1970s, when our boys were just small. It took place during winter when keeping our runway cleared of snowdrifts for safe use was always a struggle, considering how many windstorms we get along the Arctic coast. We had a tractor that Jim used to blade the runway smooth after a big blow, but I didn't know how to drive it. This led to one ironic incident when Jim had flown our Cessna 206 to Fairbanks for maintenance. I and the little boys were left home alone. Jim expected to be gone only a couple of days.

The runway was in good shape when he left, but weather delays held Jim up longer than he'd expected and while he was gone, we had a big windstorm that created hard, deep snow drifts across much of the runway. With no mechanical means to remove the snow and make the runway safe again for Jim's return, I had to use a shovel and small hand-sled to clear the snow off the runway in an area that I discerned as critical. I spent many hours of back-breaking shoveling to remove the wind-encrusted snow, piling one shovelful at a time onto the little sled until it could hold no more, and then dragging it off the runway to dump. I even worked in the middle of the night while the boys were tucked in bed. I felt proud and relieved to finally have a section I felt was enough runway cleared when news came that Jim was on his way home.

I watched him fly over and check out the runway. On his second pass, I knew he was coming in to land. To my amazement, he overflew the section I had worked so hard on and then touched down in a little area between snowdrifts further down the runway. I was devastated. Of course, I had no way of knowing that the wind would be blowing hard that day and Jim would need little runway to plop the plane down easily in a small space. In the excitement of having him home, I didn't mention my shoveling ordeal right off. But later, I complained about all my hard work going unused. It was a funny joke to everyone else, but it took a long time before I could smile over the irony of the situation.

Ironic Incidents

One fall when Jim was gone to town to have the float gear switched out for wheels on our C-206, I was left home alone to care for everything on our homesite right when we were nearing freeze-up. Some fall-time jobs had been done and Jim was due to be back home before I would need to worry about getting the last boat pulled from the water and other pre-winter tasks—or so we thought.

However, we were suddenly hit with an early drop in temperatures and one boat with a large engine on the transom was still in the water. I took it upon myself to pull it out before it froze completely in. The aluminum boat itself was not too heavy for me to pull up on the water's edge, but with the heavy motor, I couldn't budge it. After chopping the ice away from the edges of the boat and trying to lever it up any way I could, I finally had to use a come-along to slowly work it up out of the water. It was hours of work, but I succeeded.

It stayed below freezing for several days, and I was glad I'd made the effort to extract the boat from the deepening grip of ice. However, by the time Jim got home, the temperatures came back up and all the ice melted away. We ended up having a late freeze-up instead. Oh, the irony of another episode of hard work that proved unnecessary, but how was I to know? Jim's usual comment, "See, I told you so; you worry too much. You should have just waited and let it go! Humph!"

Another somewhat similar incident occurred the opposite time of year when Jim was again gone. This time it was a spring thaw scenario. The river was flooding earlier than usual, but there were still places I could drive the snowmachine on the ice—or so I thought as I did some hauling chores. As I drove by a certain spot near a pocket of water flooding in over the grounded ice, I misjudged the distance and the big wooden sled I was pulling skidded around and dropped down into some slush and stuck fast. I made several attempts to pull the sled out, but finally gave up, unhooked it, and left it there about fifty feet offshore in the slush. Later that day, as water just kept flooding in and temperatures remained well above freezing, I decided to make sure the sled was secure from floating away or somehow being crushed when the ice started moving. I put on my waterproof hip boots and carefully made my way out across the slippery water-covered ice to the sled carrying a long rope. I tied the rope to the sled and then walked back and tied the other end of the rope to a secure post on land. Phew, I figured it was safe now, and Jim and I together could pull it out later!

The irony was that all my struggles to protect the sled were for naught. Not because the sled was damaged but because days later, Jim simply drove his snowmachine out on the solidly frozen ice, chopped the sled loose, hooked it up, and towed it back to land. All the flooding on the ice had completely re-frozen and it was days later before the actual break-up flooding started again.

Without a doubt, weather remains one of the most significant influences on our remote lifestyle and one we have learned to respect. When people ask me what I predict the weather will be in the days ahead, I've learned to say, "Sure, it will be UNPREDICTABLE!"

Chapter 10
Haul Road Adventures

What About the Roads?

We have made many trips up and down the roads between Prudhoe Bay and Fairbanks, a distance of over five hundred miles. There are two major highways which traverse this north-south route north of Fairbanks, the Elliott and Dalton Highways.

The Elliott Highway was built in 1959 to connect Fairbanks with the more northern towns of Livengood and Manley Hot Springs. Mile 73 became the jumping-off point for building another road in the early 1970s to access the North Slope during the rush to market the oil newly discovered in 1968.

The Dalton Highway was built in 1974 to service the Trans-Alaska Pipeline and the Prudhoe Bay Oil Field. This is the northern route that gives access to the forty-eight-inch pipeline carrying oil from the North Slope to Valdez. The nickname Haul Road became prominent, as thousands of eighteen-wheelers and other transport vehicles traveled north over forested hills with amazing vistas, across vast wilderness, and down into valleys filled with bogs and streams. They crossed the mighty Yukon River and wound through incredibly wild land into the Brooks Range. Vehicles crossed over Atigun Pass, the highest year-round maintained pass in Alaska at 4,739 feet, and continued on through the wilderness down the north side of the Brooks Range.

From here the road gradually sloped downward to reach the coastal plain and Arctic Ocean. Road markers along the way showed the motorists that they had traveled four hundred and fourteen miles by the time they reached the end of the road in Deadhorse, Prudhoe Bay Oil Field's service center. In the beginning it was mostly a gravel road fraught with chuck holes and rough washboard surfaces in summer and dangerous ice and snowy surfaces in winter. There were and still are few services. Many signs warn drivers of everything from steep grades to avalanches. However, much has changed over the years as road maintenance has improved and some paving has been added. What hasn't changed is the dramatic scenery, including wildlife viewing and long hours of driving.

Once we got our first truck and had access to the road system via the Kuparuk road system in the mid-1980s, we were able to start making the trek up and down the route to and from Fairbanks ourselves. At first the road was closed to the public and only people contracted to the petroleum industry or other agencies were allowed access. Our family gained permitted access early on since we were both North Slope residents and operated businesses on the slope. However, by 1994, the Haul Road was opened to the public for its entire route, and permitting requirements were suspended.

I had became our family's designated driver, since Jim was the family pilot. I have many stories of adventures and incidents along the highways between home on the Colville River and Fairbanks. At least twice I drove all the way to Anchorage and back home to the Colville, an over two-thousand-mile total round-trip, which I spread out over several weeks, as I spent extra time in each town.

I have made the trip by myself in both winter and summer, but usually I have had one or two of my sons along with me. During the early years when the boys were quite young, they were along more for company for "Mom," but as the boys grew up, they also accompanied me as helpers and relief drivers. We bought a canopy for over the truck bed and a double-axle flatbed trailer to increase our capacity to haul supplies.

Fantastic scenery was a given any time of year, especially for a prairie family who had no trees or mountains around our Colville River home. The foothills, mountains, and forests

Northbound Haul Road trip in May 1987 with trailer and truck loaded with supplies and new radio tower sections.

were exciting to experience. There was a special mountain between Atigun Pass and Coldfoot that the boys and I named Rock Mountain when we first saw it, only to learn later it was a famous 4,459-foot peak already named Sukakpak Mountain. However, it forever remained Rock Mountain to us, in all its massive bare-rock glory, with one huge projection leaning toward the highway as we drove by. We have picked berries at many stops, camped in beautiful fields covered in flowers, fished for grayling in a few streams, and became familiar with all the major points of interest, such as Finger Mountain, Gobblers Knob, and the best pull-offs.

After the Dalton Highway opened for public access as far as Disaster Creek north of Coldfoot in 1981, braver, adventurous travelers began experiencing the Haul Road. When the road opened all the way to Deadhorse in 1994, the state began making improvements for travelers by constructing more public camp and rest-stop facilities along the way. Although it is still a wild and remote drive, the trip now seems tamed since we began driving it in the 1980s.

Driving the Haul Road still has its many risks and dangers. Winter brings extreme cold, snow, icy roads, blizzards, and avalanche perils. Summer travel means one could encounter heat in the nineties Fahrenheit, torrential rains and washouts, hordes of mosquitoes, and terribly dusty and rough roads. Overall, the biggest hazard year-round for us in the early days was the remoteness of this highway. There were few services and drivers had to be prepared to manage most difficulties themselves, to be self-sufficient. I always carried two spare tires for both my truck and the trailer. I had extra engine oil, transmission fluid, and other parts I might need. Survival gear was a must, such as food and camping gear.

A trip south usually started with loading sacks of frozen fish, a drive across the ice to Oliktok in order to access the Kuparuk road system, and then a drive several hours to Deadhorse. I usually spent a night there getting my fuel and travel supplies organized. Our old truck had a small fuel tank which required at least two refuels along the way. Only two places had fuel, Coldfoot and at the Yukon Bridge, and it was very expensive. So we purchased all our fuel at each end of the trip and carried extra fuel with us, plus the means to accomplish the fueling somewhere along the remote road. I usually had about thirty extra gallons in a drum or jerry jugs and a hand-operated fuel pump.

Typically, I divided the average fourteen-hour driving time in half between two days, stopping about halfway at the little community of Wiseman, a town established orginally as a small gold mining town. I dropped off fish to a dog-musher family there or at the midway truck stop called Coldfoot. Many times, the evening stop was spent in a sleeping bag in the truck. During extreme cold of winter, I had to restart the engine and warm up people and truck multiple times a night.

On the northbound leg of a trip, I always had a truck and trailer load of supplies to bring home. This was the more hazardous part of a trip for traveling with a heavy load over such rough roads was hard on equipment, especially my trailer. The truck struggled up the long grades and I had to take the long downhill grades even slower to keep careful control of my heavy trailer. I used the clutch so as not to burn up my brakes. I also had an extra braking system installed for my trailer.

Over the years of making these trips, many of the usual truck drivers got to know me, recognized my truck, and watched out for me. The drivers of the eighteen-wheelers referred to my little pickup as a four-wheeler. We all had CB radios in our vehicles and visited back and forth. My call sign was "Arctic Girl."

Truckers relayed road and weather conditions behind them to passing vehicles heading into those conditions. During winter's extreme cold, drivers would often pass on information about where the warmest pull-offs were located if I needed to stop soon. These pull-offs were invariably at the higher elevations along the road which had temperatures warmer than the lower areas. It was preferable to stop to rest or fuel up the truck where temperatures were the warmest available.

Headlights Out

A good example of an unexpected hazard was one trip where I was cruising along the bumpy road with only my headlights marking a narrow path of light in a dark, winter world. I had not seen another vehicle for hours. All of a sudden, the world went pitch black. I barely got stopped from careening off the road's edge. There I sat wondering what had happened. How could both headlights burn out at once?

I finally remembered being told about all the little fuses under the dash that connected all the wires to the electrical system. Maybe I should check those. I had a little kit of spare fuses of all sizes in my glove box. I found the fuses under the dash and with a flashlight, looked for one that looked blown, since I had no idea which wires went to which systems. Sure enough, there was one fuse with a tiny metal strip broken in two. Not good. I matched a good breaker by number and replaced the good for bad. Voilà, my lights came back on! What a relief. I drove on.

Winter Storms Conditions

One winter when I was northbound pulling a heavily loaded trailer, I ran into a severe windstorm. Not only was visibility obscured to only a few feet, but blowing snow was being driven into deep drifts across the road. I had to creep along, carefully

*Northbound Haul Road headed to our Colville homesite in March, 1987,
crossing the Chandalar Shelf approaching Atigun Pass, elevation 4,739
feet, towing a trailer laden with lumber and a new canoe.*

watching the road markers along the side to be able to stay
on the road. It was true whiteout conditions and getting more
and more dangerous. Finally, I couldn't keep my speed up
enough to break through the continually building snowdrifts.
I had to pull over and stop. About then I saw lights coming
up behind me. An eighteen-wheeler materialized out of the
whiteout, slowed down, and then a voice boomed over my CB
radio, "Hey, little four-wheeler, pull in behind me and I'll break
trail for you!"

"Will do! Thanks!" I answered as I pulled out and stuck to
him like glue. All I could see were two little red, bouncing
taillights ahead of me, but I was able to follow them all the
remaining way to Deadhorse. As I said, most of those drivers
of the big rigs were very kind and thoughtful to me.

Another severe storm experience I had was on a southbound
trip. It had been snowing for miles and I was slowed way down
by poor visibility when we reached the bottom of a long, steep
grade named the Beaver Slide. I had seen no traffic for some
time, yet I called ahead on my CB radio, asking if any traffic
was coming down the Beaver Slide. I received an answer from
someone sitting at the pull-off at the top of the hill telling me
that all rigs were pulled off waiting for the weather to improve.

With that, I decided to drive on, but soon visibility dropped so drastically I could no longer see either side of the road. There was no place to get off the road and remaining stopped in the middle of the road was even more dangerous, just in case another vehicle tried coming down, or even up. I had to go on. I had Jay, the oldest of the three boys with me that trip, bundle up and get out and walk ahead of the truck. From outside of the truck, he could see the road edges better than I could and lead me exactly up the middle. I could just see him through the windshield to follow close behind. We inched our way up the hill, and, boy, was I relieved when the grade finally began to flatten out and the pull-off materialized out of the swirling snow. There were several big trucks parked there. I didn't talk to any of the drivers, but they probably thought, "That crazy woman!"

Summer Travels

Summer travel's biggest danger was road washouts from rainstorms. Several of the boys and I were southbound late one August when rain began to devastate the Haul Road in several critical places, including both north and south of Atigun Pass. I had carefully driven through a rushing stream of water that had overflowed its normal path and was transecting a section of road just before starting the final ascent to the top of Atigun Pass. Later I learned that the road experienced a complete collapse at this spot, and I was the last vehicle over the pass that day.

A little while later, I was stopped at another wash-out as a creek undercut the road a few miles north of Wiseman. As we waited several hours, road equipment feverishly worked to create a detour around the problem. Finally, we were able to creep across a temporary bridge over the wildly tumbling water pouring across what used to be the road. On we drove in the pouring rain.

Unfortunately, our troubles weren't over. Just past Coldfoot, we were stopped again by road crews repairing yet another, even worse, wash-out. We were told that it would take hours of repairs before traffic could get through, so we returned to

Coldfoot for the night. Meanwhile, I called a friend and asked if he could fly up and pick up Jay at the nearby runway to take him on to Fairbanks so he wouldn't be late to his first day of college. "Yes," was the answer.

However, to get over to the runway, I had to drive across another flooding creek that ran parallel to the main road. Water was deep and swift and without knowing the condition of the road under the swirling water, I was hesitant to blindly cross the estimated one hundred feet. Jay came to my rescue by volunteering to guide me across by wearing hip boots and using a strong stick for support. He carefully made his way across the water by checking back and forth to verify solid ground beneath and I slowly followed behind him. Thanks to our friend Jon, who flew through some pretty rough and stormy weather to make it in and out of the Coldfoot valley, Jay made it to Fairbanks safely. Two days later, we finally made it to town also.

Because we always replaced tires often, I almost never had a flat tire on my truck. The only time I remember was once on a southbound trip due to a helpful mechanic overfilling my tires before I left Deadhorse. That was not the case with the small double axel trailer I often towed. I almost

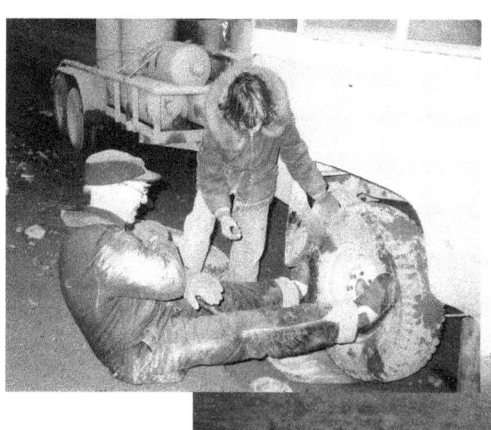

Teena's only flat tire on her truck over all the years driving in the far north.

never made a trip without one or more flats at least on the northbound leg when the trailer was heavily loaded. We were traversing hundreds of miles of the roughest, most remote wilderness in the state. Tires took a tremendous beating.

I had friends at the Jim River Maintenance Station and they helped me out quite often. One year I was northbound, towing a trailer laden with lumber, full one-hundred-pound propane bottles, other supplies, and a new canoe strapped on top, when I looked back in my mirror and realized the trailer had a flat tire on the back axle. I quickly pulled over as far off the road as I could get and stopped. As I got out and began to walk back, the trailer groaned and tilted sideways as two more tires flattened on the opposite side. Oh, no! I had only two spare trailer tires and now three flats at once. What was I going to do?

We had just passed the Jim River Maintenance Camp about ten miles back down the road. I remembered my friends there and hoped they could help me. Leaving Derek, who was with me on this particular trip, to stay with our rig, I hitchhiked back down the road to the road maintenance camp. Al and Sandy were there, and Al quickly came up with a plan. He took a wheel off his old jeep that sat out in the field near their trailer-house. It was just the right size and together we returned to my truck. Derek had already started changing the flat tires so getting all three flats changed out went quickly. Thanks, Al! You saved the day again! It wasn't the first time he had helped with trailer problems.

As we continued north, I worried about the distance I still had to go, now with no spares for the trailer. I decided to stop at Coldfoot, about thirty miles on ahead, to see if I could get my best flat tire repaired. Fortunately, I was able to round up a mechanic who was able to fix one tire. That was a big relief, and I continued on with more confidence. After another two hundred and forty plus miles over the extremely rough road, and no more flats, we reached Deadhorse. I replaced the borrowed wheel with another good one and sent Al's wheel back to him with a trucker friend who was just heading south.

On another fall-time trip, I was returning my parents to Fairbanks after a summer visit on the Colville. Jay was along with us and we four were crammed in together in my little truck cab on the long drive to town. We were about halfway and nearing the Jim River Maintenance Station in a torrential downpour that had been hampering my driving for hours. I knew our friends were up ahead and we planned to stop for the night there.

However, the descending darkness, insistent rain, and my exhaustion finally convinced me to stop sooner. I pulled off onto a little side road and we sat there deciding what to do. I had lost track of exactly how close we were to our planned stop, so we decided to hang there for the night. Dad removed gear from the back of the truck and put a tarp over the pile to repel the worst of the rain. He and Mom made themselves as comfortable as possible in sleeping bags inside the canopy covering the truck bed and Jay found a little place in back, too. I curled up on the seat in the front. Rain fell all night.

The next morning, we loaded up again and continued on. We were surprised to learn that our intended stop was only a few miles on down the road. "Oh, well! Better safe than sorry," I moaned. We were quite a bedraggled crew knocking on the Woodward's door but were welcomed warmly and were soon treated to a wonderful visit with yummy breakfast included.

Scary Vehicular Incidents

A few vehicular incidents occurred, but we never had any serious accidents over the years. Problems were mostly with my trailer. I've had many flat tires, some broken springs, and had my hitch break and nearly lost the trailer over the edge of an embankment. I've had to chain up one side of a damaged back axle on my trailer twice and limp onward on three wheels until I could reach a shop. I lost a brand-new tire off my trailer one time when the whole wheel flew off the brake drum and rolled out into some muskeg never to be found. Fortunately, all these episodes were challenges, but nothing life threatening.

However, one incident was very nearly serious. Jay and I were northbound with only our loaded truck, no trailer. Jay was driving and as he was just exiting a narrow bridge, he hit a spot of black ice. He was slowed down since bridges are notoriously slick, but even so, the truck suddenly went out of control and made a 360° spin in the middle of the road. Thank goodness there was no oncoming traffic. Before we knew it, the truck was making a second 360°, but this time it came to a jarring halt with a big crashing noise. It happened so fast we were stunned. The truck was facing forward on the very edge of an eighteen-foot precipice, and we could feel the right back end tilted down over the edge. I reached over and pulled the emergency parking brake and then we gently climbed out of the cab on the driver's side. It was a three-foot snow berm that had stopped us with such force that it knocked the whole back end off our truck canopy and ejected half our load down into the ravine filled with three to four-feet deep snow. Debris was sticking out of the snow everywhere. The canopy back was nowhere to be seen.

We needed to get the truck back to level ground on the road first but were apprehensive to try moving the truck in case it slipped further over the edge. About then a big eighteen-wheeler rig drove by us and pulled over.

"Hi, folks, do you need some help?" the trucker asked as he walked back to us.

"Yes," I boldly answered, "we need help getting the truck safely back on the road."

He confidently hooked a chain to both vehicles and pulled us up with little effort from his big rig. He kindly mentioned that I needed to release the parking brake now and keep it off, since it tends to freeze up in extreme cold temperatures. I thanked him kindly for the advice and for helping us, and that we could take it from there. He was soon on his way north again.

It took several hours to retrieve our load. It was hard work digging through the deep snow in the ravine to locate our gear and drag it back up the steep bank. The most difficult task was our thirty-gallon poly drum full of gas. We struggled with it for a long time. It was just too heavy to lift and carry up the slippery hill. Finally, with Jay pulling on a rope and me pushing from below, we managed to maneuver it back up onto the road. We decided to pump as much fuel as we could into the truck tank to lighten the drum before lifting it back into the truck.

I scooted one last time down the bank into the snow to see if I could find anything we had missed recovering. As I thrashed a little further out than before, my shin hit something hard, and I had found the missing back to the canopy. It had rocketed down and under the distant snow like a missile. Jay had to help pull it up. Amazingly, it was not damaged, but fit right back on the truck perfectly. Apparently, the force of our impact had bowed the back outward just enough to pop it out of its slide-bolt clasps. With the door back in place, we were finally on our way again, being ever more careful of the icy roads.

Wildlife Encounters on Haul Road

We have experienced many wildlife sightings and encounters over the years while traveling on the Haul Road as it winds along next to Alaska's oil pipeline. Wildlife always adds enjoyment and anticipation to the long hours of driving. We have watched moose, caribou, muskoxen, foxes, lynx, wolves, wolverines, Dall sheep, snowshoe rabbits, porcupines, Arctic ground squirrels, and many species of small birds plus big birds like ptarmigan, owls, and hawks. The most excitement is undoubtedly bear encounters.

One time, Aaron and I stopped at the pull-off by the Atigun River Bridge to gas the truck up. This had become almost a regular stop for us over the years as we head south on the Haul Road, since it is usually where we are about out of gas after driving the first three hundred and fifty miles south out of Deadhorse. We are into the northern edge of the Brooks Range by then and the road follows the oil pipeline quite closely through the valley that leads to Atigun Pass. The scenery is spectacular through this area.

I had agreed to let Aaron try fishing in the river below the bridge for a few minutes. We needed a break from the long hours in the truck. We had no sooner reached the edge of the small, tumultuous river when I looked up to see a big grizzly looking at us from a very short distance away between some tall willow bushes. My heart began to race, but I calmly told Aaron to come with me back up to the road, and we walked, not ran, back to the truck that was parked a short distance

Two stragglers from a nearby herd of muskoxen along the Haul Road.

away. Once we were back inside the relative safety of the vehicle, I looked back to see where the bear was located. It took a minute to find her, but she was walking away with a yearling cub at her side, just crossing under the huge pipe. A mother with a cub is more dangerous than ever, but the cub must have been hidden by the bushes when I first saw the bigger bear, so I wasn't burdened with that added detail as we made our retreat. Aaron, only six, was quite unconcerned once I had explained to him why we had to return to the truck. I had been calm and hid my initial alarm. Aaron still didn't think it had been necessary to abandon the river's edge just because of a bear.

He said, "Mom, all we needed to do is tell the bear our names and then it wouldn't have bothered us."

I have no idea where Aaron came up with this solution, but I do know he had heard a lot of bear stories from family members and did not really fear them.

Another time many years after that episode, we had another grizzly bear experience at almost the same spot. This time it was my eighteen-year-old son Jay with me. Again, we had stopped to fuel up the truck and Jay asked for a little time to hike up to the top of a nearby ridge he had been wanting to climb for years. We had to wait for another vehicle traveling with us to catch up, so Jay had time to exercise his legs. He was only a speck against the sky when he reached the top. I could only find him with the binoculars. Then he started back down. It was about then that I noticed a large grizzly bear strolling along just under the pipeline across the road from me, a distance of several hundred yards. I enjoyed watching the bear, but then realized that Jay's route down from the ridge was very likely to intercept the bear's route. Sure enough, they kept getting closer and closer. I got out of the truck and waved my arms at Jay trying to get his attention to no avail. Jay just kept coming and the bear kept moseying along. Both were unconcerned.

The bear passed on by in front of Jay, and soon Jay crossed under the pipe and was back to the truck, totally unaware of the drama I had been watching. He had never even noticed the bear as he had hurried back to the truck. From his vantage point higher on the hill, he had seen our companion vehicle coming in the distance and was only concerned with getting back to the truck quickly. Jay laughed at my concern, but Mother Bear has a right to feel protective of her cub.

I had several funny wildlife-related episodes traveling the Haul Road with my brother-in-law Richard and sister Marti in 2009. Richard went with me south and Marti on the northbound trip.

Richard and I were about thirty miles south of Deadhorse when we pulled off the road onto a pipeline access and gated spur to the pipeline that is normally locked to keep unauthorized travelers out. It happened to be open for road maintenance equipment to haul water from a small lake inside the gate. We had spotted a herd of muskoxen a short distance away along the Sagavanirktok River and Richard wanted to photograph them. I drove as far down the spur road as I could to get as close to the muskoxen as possible and stopped in a cluster of tall willow bushes. While Richard stalked the animals with his camera, I studied the many wildflowers strewn all around. Such beauty! Time got away from us. It was evening before we realized we needed to be on our way.

Unfortunately, when we returned to the gate back out to the main road, it was closed! No one had known we were inside, and the equipment operators had quit and locked the gate for the night. These narrow access roads are constructed in such a way as to discourage or prevent anyone from driving around the gate, using big rocks to block the way or steep shoulders on the four to five-foot-tall road surface. It appeared we were stuck there for the night. Being stubborn, reluctant to give in, I decided I could drive around anyway. I put the truck in low-wheel drive and with Richard carefully directing me, I crept over the sloped side of the road, tipped at an alarming angle, and inched my way along past the locked gate. It was scary, but I made it! That is one muskox herd we won't forget.

On the return trip with my sister, we encountered Dall sheep in the mountains and muskoxen on the tundra that she wanted to photograph. I took a nap while Marti climbed a steep hillside to get pictures of sheep she could almost touch. Later, at another stop, I had to call out a warning to her to get back from an angry-looking muskox cow that was only a few feet behind her. I was relieved that we saw no nearby bears that trip. I was afraid she would insist on more close-up photography. Phew!

On a trip Isaac and I made to Fairbanks in 2016, we were able to get up close and personal to a huge bull moose feeding beside the highway not far from the Yukon River. There is so much wilderness to traverse on a Haul Road trip that the wildlife and beautiful scenery seems never ending.

A Special Life

I've always felt special, and I don't mean in an arrogant or boastful way, but in a different way. Yes, I know I am special and loved by God, but I have also felt that God chose me for a very special kind of life that entailed both wonderful adventure and uniqueness, but also trials and hardship, a life requiring courage, strength and perseverance. God didn't toss me into this life without preparation. He gave me a rugged constitution, and an easy-going personality that could take most anything life threw at me with calm courage.

I was born into a unique family with adventuresome and dedicated parents who transported their family to the northern edge of the United States to live and work among the friendly and industrious Iñupiat people, as they faced the arduous struggle to acclimate to the encroaching civilization. This involved a life that was always intriguing to "outside" people, giving me that first awareness of being special.

Then, I survived and recovered from a terrible disease that often left victims crippled and dependent on others—Polio. Although I still have weaknesses and some minor disabilities, 1 knew I was truly blessed when I recovered relatively good health and resumed life with strength and resilience.

When I married into the Helmericks family, my "specialness" jumped again, for this family had become famous for a unique and independent life clawed out of a harsh environment on the edge of the Arctic Ocean. My father-in-law had become a famous adventurer and explorer across the Arctic regions. He authored books about these travels, became a renowned bush pilot and guide, and shared his Arctic expertise with the many newcomers to Alaska's North Slope.

My husband, Jim, followed in his father's footsteps and I was soon drawn into this adventurous life. However, it was a life requiring me to live a rough and tumble, frontier-woman-style existence, which meant hard work, isolation, learning new skills, and helping to build our home that has served three generations of our family. I've had a life of great freedom and independence, but also one of many struggles and hardships, family-based conflicts, and having to navigate stormy weather along the way, both literally and figuratively.

Through it all, I have always had confidence that I was where I belonged and was always supported by God who put me here and promised to give me whatever I needed to persevere and even thrive through all the ups and downs of my special life.

Afterward

Life on the Colville River continues. It has been fifty-three years in June of 2023 since I traveled to the northern edge of Alaska with my new husband, Jim, to carve out a home and life on the edge of the Arctic Ocean. I resummed prairie life and became reacquainted with joys and challenges of the high Arctic—missed since my childhood.

I look back on all the years and know the stories in this book catch only a small part of my storehouse of memories, both in my mind and daily journals. I pick up old journals and start reading and soon I'm sucked into long-forgotten events, exclaiming to Jim over and over, "Wow, I don't remember that! Do you remember when we . . . ?"

Our world has changed drastically over the years since our homesite was first settled by Jim and his parents in the mid-1950s. Except for a few transient Iñupiat families, we were the only ones living permanently within the hundreds of miles between Utqiaġvik, Alaska's northernmost point to the west of us, and Kaktovik on Barter Island, near the Canadian border to the east of us. Other than a few lights on the horizon to the northeast from the DEW Line station, there was nothing man-made visible in any direction from our house. We were truly isolated and living in a wilderness few others saw besides our own family and guests.

Once the exploration and retrieval of oil started, changes exploded rapidly. More lights were visible, and permanent roads began advancing toward us from the east which opened up more options for travel and obtaining supplies. However, the growing oil field changed little of our scenery or activities right here at our Colville Homesite in those early days.

What brought the most noticeable changes in our local area of the Colville River Delta was the creation of a new native village about twenty-two miles upriver from us. It was only a few families at first, but eventually grew into a community of over four hundred people. We had new neighbors and the land had to adapt to the increased traffic of winter vehicles, summer boats, aircraft, and the increased pressure in hunting and fishing. We witnessed decreases in numbers and changes in wildlife patterns around the Colville River Delta area. Increases in human habitation and activities affect any land, and the encroaching oil field added to this impact as they spread west into the Delta and even further west. Additionally, a newly-formed local government with its ensuing taxes and regulations added another new element to our previously isolated life.

Many of my stories in this book reflect these changes which brought both advantages and disadvantages. We experienced positive changes like new supply and travel routes, better communications systems, a closer Post Office, expanded job opportunities, new firewood sources, increased business, and

Teena at work in the oil field.

Teena on bear guard duty, where she worked with field biological studies and survey crews.

friendly visitors and neighbors. On the other hand, we have suffered increasing disturbances in traffic, noise, lights, and visual pollution. As the oil field moved west, we not only had lights much closer, but the buildings, rigs, and power lines gradually covered most of our eastern landscape, including drill sites within just a few miles of our island home. Then the oil and gas industry moved past us and now lights and visible infrastructure are within sight to the west of us, too.

In general, we have had favorable impressions of the oil industry's stewardship of the land here on the North Slope. They have many federal, state, and local environmental guidelines and stipulations with which to comply, but from our experience, they also go above and beyond to safely and responsibly operate in this fragile environment.

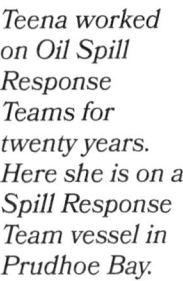

Teena worked on Oil Spill Response Teams for twenty years. Here she is on a Spill Response Team vessel in Prudhoe Bay.

Other changes came along for our family. Besides caring for home, family, schooling, farm animals and guests on our homesite over the many years, I began working on various oil field jobs in the early 2000s. The kids were grown and gone, and extra income was welcome since remote life is expensive. My jobs have included managing logistics, expediting supplies, coordinating air travel, participating in oil spill response activities, supporting field environment crews, and managing remote exploration camps.

Our land is like an island of wilderness, a special protected spot or wildlife sanctuary that is home to hundreds of birds and other wildlife. The land has remained unchanged even though our living conditions have evolved from small tents to modern homes. Despite the many changes all around us, we still love and hang on to our independent life carved out of a harsh but beautiful land.

Jim and Teena standing underneath the museum's mounts of a caribou family in the upstairs Greatroom.

Teena and Jim with their four grown sons, left to right, Derek, Jay, Isaac, and Aaron in the Colville home, spring 2018.

Appendix and Index

In memory of our sweet Ruby who shared her love and boundless devotion with us for so many years.
7/4/2009 – 8/13/2023

We miss you dearly!

Appendix

Iñupiaq Terms

Qaaqtaq – (kaaq'– tuk) Name for Arctic Cisco whitefish.

Quaq – (kwaak) Raw, frozen fish or meat.

Auruq – (our-uck) Soured/pickled fish.

Akutuq – (ah'-koo-tuk) Eskimo "ice-cream" made with whipped animal fat (usually caribou fat) and often added berries.

Aanaakliq (Anachlik) – (ah-nock'-lick) Broad Whitefish (*Coregonus nasus*); also, the name of the island on which the Helmericks homestead is located in the Colville River Delta. This Iñupiaq word had a spelling change as the written language developed, but the spelling remained "Anachlik" on formal maps already in existence, and I use this earlier spelling as we knew it at the time the text was written in this book.

Anachlik – (ah-nock'-lick) Name of island in Colville River Delta and Iñupiaq name for Broad Whitefish used in earlier years before spelling changes.

Iñupiat – (Ĭ-nu-pee-ut) The indigenous people (mostly Alaskan) whose traditional territory spans northeast from the Norton Sound to the northernmost part of the Canadian-United States.

Iñupiaq – (Ĭ-nu-pee-ck) Language traditionally spoken by the Iñupiat (indigenous) people whose homeland spans from Norton Sound to the northeast boundary of Alaska and Canada.

Pivsi –(piv'-see) Dried whitefish, often smoked.

Maktak – (muck-tuck) (formerly spelled muktuk) Whale meat, usually outer black skin with some blubber attached.

Glossary

Antler velvet – The soft, fur-like skin that encases antlers as they grow.

Arctic Cisco – *Coregonus antumnalis*, an anadromous (meaning it spawns in freshwater, but can feed and overwinter in saltwater) species of freshwater whitefish, caught in nets with Helmericks fishing operations. The Iñupiaq spelling is "aanaakliq."

Backhaul – Act of hauling freight or supplies on return trip or the materials transported on a return trip.

Break-up – The process of a frozen river in spring changing to free-flowing water. A river will begin thawing from its winter frozen state, with ice melting, breaking up and being pushed down-river and out to sea by high levels of spring melt water, often causing ice jams and flooding.

Bush – Referring to wilderness and remote areas away from populated areas.

Come-along – A common name for a hand-operated ratchet lever winch, which is a mechanical device used to wind a rope or cable while using a ratchet to keep the line from unwinding—used to move heavy object.

Ice cellar – A shaft dug ten to thirty feet into the frozen ground or permafrost to keep food frozen. They have covers or lids and ladders that descend down into the shafts to access the freezing area below. Sometimes structures are built over the top of the cellars—as with all our cellars— for convenience and protection. Our cellars also have side tunnels at the bottom for extra storage space in order to accommodate our large volume of commercial fish, which is kept frozen even in the summer.

Ice Road – A road created during winter for transportation across frozen tracks of land and ice (sea-ice or lakes) beyond existing roads, usually for exploration purposes, made by laying down water and ice-chips in layers to freeze until a road with sufficient depth of strong supporting ice is created. This road then melts in summer, leaving little damage to the fragile landscape.

Muskeg – A peat bog formed by sphagnum moss, leaves, and decayed matter.

Overflow – Liquid water on top of frozen lake, sea, or river ice in winter, due to water pressure (rain, strong tides from high winds) building up under the ice, forcing it to break out and accumulate on top of the ice. Dangerous for travelers if they get stuck or wet in freezing conditions.

Permafrost – Ground that stays permanently frozen year-round. Made up of soil and rocks as well as frozen water, permafrost forms when the depth of winter freezing exceeds the depth of summer thawing, thus creating ground that never has a chance to thaw even during the warm summer months.

Sastrugi – (zastrugi) Sharp, angular grooves or ridges formed on a snow surface by wind erosion, common in cold, windy regions, shaped much like frozen waves.

Snowmachine – A motorized, tracked machine used in snow conditions for travel and recreation. Also known as a snowmobile.

Snow Trail – Winter roads or trails made on ice surfaces (lakes, rivers, and sea-ice) by plowing snow off intended route to enable mobile equipment to travel off-road without becoming stuck in deep snow.

Supply Run – Travel intended to get supplies (often including mail).

Whiteout – Atmospheric and surface conditions causing extremely limited visibility (usually down to zero-zero) due to sky and landscape blending together, creating a white world with no horizon and no shadows.

Locations

Anachlik Island – The island in the eastern Colville River Delta, Alaska, on which the Helmericks Homesite is located. The Iñupiaq name was revised with a different spelling to "Aanaakliq" in recent years, but the original spelling remains on most maps.

Barrow – The name of the northernmost community in the United States from the early 1800s until 2016, when the town voted to change its name to its original Iñupiaq name of Utqiaġvik.

Coldfoot – A small community first established in 1974 as a truck stop for vehicles traversing the 414 miles of the Dalton Highway (nicknamed Haul Road), which connects Fairbanks to the Prudhoe Bay Oil Field by the Arctic Ocean. Coldfoot is found at Mile 175 along the Highway, is on the south side of the Brooks Range, and lies in the valley with the Middle Fork of the Koyukuk River.

Colville Village – Secondary name used for the extensive Helmericks Homesite compound.

Dalton Highway – Also known as the Haul Road, the highway from Elliott Highway north of Fairbanks to Deadhorse.

Deadhorse – The industrial service area for the Greater Prudhoe Bay Oil Field complex on Alaska's North Slope, which includes the commercial Deadhorse Airport. It is the terminus of the Haul Road.

Dinosaur Bar – A family name given a large sandbar on the Colville River about thirty-five miles upriver from the Helmericks Homesite on which temporary research camps were established to excavate dinosaur fossils along the Colville River bluffs.

Haul Road – Common name for the Dalton Highway.

Homestead/Homesite – Although our land on Anachlik Island was originally filed as a Homestead under the Federal Homestead Act, it was ultimately proved-up as two Trade & Manufacturing sites instead. Even though the name "Homestead" stuck over the years, I usually refer to our land as our "homesite" to be more accurate.

Kalubik Creek – A creek that drains into Harrison Bay along the eastern coastline between the Colville Delta and Oliktok Point.

Kuparuk – The second largest oil field on the North Slope of Alaska, west of Prudhoe Bay and between the Kuparuk and Colville Rivers.

Kuparuk River – River between the Colville and Sagavanirktok (Sag, for short) Rivers on Alaska's North Slope.

Milne Point – Point of land along the edge of the Arctic Ocean between Oliktok Point and the Kuparuk River Delta.

Naval Arctic Research Laboratory (NARL) – An Arctic Research station run by the U.S. Navy from the 1940s to the 1980s, located near Barrow.

Nigliq – New spelling for Niglik. The name for the far western Colville River Delta channel and for the summer fish camp.

North Slope – Extensive region of northern Alaska that slopes downward from the Brooks Range to the coastline of the Arctic Ocean and extends from the western edge of Alaska bordering the Chukchi Sea to the northeastern side edging the Beaufort Sea.

Nuiqsut – An Eskimo village first established in 1973 (incorporated as a city in 1975), at the head of the Colville River Delta, located about one hundred and thirty-six miles southeast of Utqiaġvik, and twenty-two miles upriver from Helmericks Homesite.

Ocean Point – A point of land about thirty miles upriver from the Colville River Delta that marks the beginning of the tall river bluffs that continue to run along the eastern side of the river for many miles.

Oliktok – A point of land on the mainland side of the northeast edge of the Colville River Delta (also known as Oliktok Point).

Pingo Beach – Helmericks name for the first beach-like shore with gravel (opposed to mud) as one travels upriver from Helmericks Homesite on the east side of the river about five miles below Ocean Point.

Prudhoe Bay – This refers to both the physical bay directly west of the Sagavanirktok River Delta at the edge of the Arctic Ocean, but is also the name given to the entire oil field that was developed in that area by the oil industry. The industrial service area and airport named Deadhorse is found within this greater operating area and is also the northern terminus of the Haul Road.

Utqiaġvik – The northernmost town in Alaska, formerly known as Barrow. The town voted to use the village's traditional Iñupiaq name in 2016. Teena's Dad, Rev. William C. Wartes, missionary/pastor of the Presbyterian Mission in the 1950s supported the church name as the "Utḳeaġvik Presbyterian Church" which is used to this day with updated spelling of Utqiaġvik.

Studies and Projects We Supported

- Animal studies including a fox study conducted through several seasons to document feeding and reproductive activities of the white Arctic fox.

- Off-shore projects including the federal Outer Continental Shelf (OCS) studies.

- The University of Alaska Fairbanks conducted many studies including several projects documenting the easterly flow of currents along the northern Alaskan coast.

- We supported work conducted by the United States Geological Service (USGS).

- Environmental companies were supported who had contracts to study the ecology of bird and fish populations across the North Slope to develop baseline information which could later be used to track the effect of the petroleum industry. This included extensive aerial wildlife surveying and also providing our own commercial fisheries data.

- We often supported the Naval Arctic Research Laboratory (NARL) from Utqiaġvik with projects they had out our way, plus supplied fish for their caged animals to eat.

- We supported and guided marine operators who were barging supplies up the Colville River for various projects and to the new village of Nuiqsut.

- We supplied lodging and support for a university study of tundra insects, also under a USGS contract.

- Jim provided aerial support for bird projects on the Barrier Islands near Utqiaġvik.

- Both state and federal wildlife agencies used our services extensively: Alaska Department of Fish & Game (ADF&G) and United States Fish & Wildlife Service (USFWS).

- We have worked for many years with projects under the National Oceanic and Atmospheric Administration (NOAA) and the National Marine Fisheries Service.

- We have also been volunteers for over twenty-five years for the NOAA National Weather Service—Alaska Region. Our daily weather reports from here on the Colville River Delta go into the national database.

- We have supported or provided consultations on all kinds of environmental issues for many oil/gas companies and their affiliate companies, like seismic operators.

- Collaboration with companies that do oil spill response and other clean-up work were often on our plates. (Teena has been on oil spill responder teams since the late 1990s.)

- Aerial support often meant picking up people and supplies from the commercial airport in Deadhorse (Prudhoe Bay) with our Cessna 206, landing here on our homestead runway, transferring to our Piper Super Cub and relaying everything to a remote field camp. One year, goods were even dropped into a field camp by a large plane with parachutes and Jim flew in with the Piper Super Cub to retrieve the parachutes so that they could be picked up later by a bigger plane at our place for use again.

- Hunters and other big game guides sometimes come to us for aid and advice about operations on the North Slope.

Index

A

B

About the Author

Teena Helmericks is a frontier woman who has lived and thrived along the edge of the Arctic coast of Alaska. After her childhood in Utqiaġvik, the northern most village in Alaska, and school years in Washington State, she then took up life on an island in the Colville River Delta where the river meets the Arctic Ocean. There her life progressed on the family's three-generation homestead-like parcel of land from meager means and extreme remoteness to modern homes and many neighbors.

Teena and her family witnessed the discovery and development of the North Slope Gas and Petroleum Industry. They observed many changes across the whole North Slope over the years as local governments formed and villages expanded along with this petroleum industry. She and her husband raised four boys who thrived on homeschooling and their frontier-style life laced with adventure, hard work, and exceptional wilderness expertise.

Articles by Teena have appeared in *Alaska: The Magazine of Life on the Last Frontier* and the *Prudhoe Bay Journal*.

www.ingramcontent.com/pod-product-compliance
Lightning Source LLC
Chambersburg PA
CBHW051508120626
46551CB00012B/821